As an Integrative... realize that there... information surro... incredibly hard for people to even know where to begin and then you lose focus on what you really want/need. "Balanced Bodies" provided me with incredibly valuable information and put me on the "straight and arrow," giving me the ability to focus on my four bodies and not only understand how they work, but also provide extremely useful and simple tools on how to effectively work towards balancing them. Walking away from reading this book made me feel like I actually have a guideline to follow in life; this book gives direction! Thank you, Alexandra, for this beautiful life-changing gift!

Danielle Silbernagel, INHC
Integrative Nutrition Health Coach
Vanskoy, Saskatchewan, Canada

As a mental health professional specializing in addiction care, I find that helping my clients understand the importance of caring equally for mind, body, and spirit in their recovery process can be a daunting task. Alexandra's book serves as a valuable growth resource to help recovering addicts/alcoholics see the importance of improving themselves as a whole rather than just simply stopping the use of a substance. The intricate web of the emotional, mental, physical, and spiritual bodies and the necessity of improving each has not been well explained at a level mental health clients of all types can easily understand... until now. Job well done!

Montica A. O'Barr, LPC-S, LCDC
Ready To Change Counseling
Waxahachie, Texas

Balanced Bodies

A holistic approach to happiness

Alexandra M. Asirvadam
LPC, LCDC, INHC

Foreword by Dr. Blake Gordon, NP
Dallas, Texas

Balanced Bodies: A holistic approach to happiness.

Copyright © 2017 by Alexandra M. Asirvadam

All rights reserved. No part of this book may be reproduced in any form or by any electronic or mechanical means, including information storage and retrieval systems, without permission in writing from the author. For information, contact Alexandra M. Asirvadam at alexandra@amacounseling.com.

The content of this book is for general informational purposes only. Each person's physical, emotional, and spiritual condition is unique. Please consult your doctor for matters pertaining to your specific physical and mental health and diet. This book is not meant to be used, nor should it be used, to diagnose or treat any medical or mental health condition or to replace the services of your physician or other healthcare provider. The advice and strategies contained in the book may not be suitable for all readers. Please consult your healthcare provider for any questions that you may have about your own medical situation. Neither the author nor publisher guarantees the accuracy of information in this book or its usefulness to a particular reader, nor are they responsible for any damage or negative consequence that may result from any treatment, action taken, or inaction by any person reading or following the information in this book.

All rights reserved. No part of this publication may be reproduced, distributed, or transmitted in any form or by any means, including photocopying, recording, or other electronic or mechanical methods, without the prior written permission of the publisher or author, except in the case of brief quotations embodied in critical reviews and certain other noncommercial uses permitted by copyright law. For permission requests, email the publisher or author at alexandra@amacounseling.com.

CHAPTER 7: Self-care in action	175
Overview of self-care ideas	177
How to start self-care	181
How to finetune and build on existing self-care	191
Conclusion	197
About the author	203
Notes	205
Resources	209
Identity – Healthy relationships – boundaries	217
Physical body/Emotional body	219
Mental body/Spiritual body	221

Contents

Dedication	9
Acknowledgments	11
Foreword	13
Introduction	17
CHAPTER 1: Moving mental health counseling to the next level	29
CHAPTER 2: The four bodies	35
CHAPTER 3: The physical body	43
How to feed your body	55
How to get your body moving	64
How to support your kids	70
CHAPTER 4: The emotional body	75
How to feel what you want to feel	85
How to support your kids	97
CHAPTER 5: The mental body	105
How to think what you want to think	133
How to support your kids	153
CHAPTER 6: The spiritual body	159
How to live your spirituality	165
How to support your kids	171

Dedication

I dedicate this book to my parents, Monika and Josef Naray, who have loved and supported me for more than four and a half decades, no matter what unexpected challenges I surprised them with. And there were many. We have laughed and cried, gone through hardships together, made it through disagreements, and butted heads, but they still love me unconditionally, and they always have. I moved to the other side of the world, and they are still here for me, doing what they can. They don't hold it against me when they don't hear from me as much as they would like to, they know how busy my life gets at times. They may also know how hard it is for me to live two lives on two different continents and that this may have to do with me not being in touch as much, in addition to the ridiculous time change of course. Distance doesn't matter, it seems. My parents are incredibly present in my life. I cannot imagine how hard it is for them that my kids and I live so far away and we cannot get those afternoon coffees in as easily as we always thought we would. Thank you for everything you have ever done. Thank you for being there for me. Thank you for loving me. I love you so much!

To contact the publisher, visit
www.amacounseling.com

To contact the author, visit
www.amacounseling.com

ISBN-13: 978-0692969915
ISBN-10: 0692969918

Library of Congress Control Number: 2017916352
AMA Counseling, Waxahachie, TX

Printed in the United States of America

Acknowledgments

I have had this dream to write a book forever. And now it's done. I want to thank everyone who played a part in getting me to this point:

My friends on the European continent, who are really part of my family: Gabi Ifkovits, my best friend of all times who gives it to me straight and supports whatever I do at the same time; Monika Hammond, who not only listens and shares her wisdom with me, encourages me, and tries to get the best out of me but also agreed to take time out of her busy schedule to edit my book; and Sylvia Tin, my soul support, whose endeavor it is to finally get me on my right path and who kept reminding me that I needed to write this book before I even knew I would ever get started.

My first friend in Texas, Dorothy Boisseau, who made this book look good inside and outside with her graphic design wisdom. Thank you so much for the time you put into this project.

My friends on the American continent, who also agreed to read through, edit, and improve this book: Erica Goldsmith, my accountability partner during my writing process; Regina Parker, my friend and bike buddy who makes me feel normal; and Bob Habasevich, I just met you, and you agreed to help me with this project too. I feel blessed.

Sara O'Barr, who took my headshots and is always ready to give me her straightforward advice about pretty much anything and everything.

My parents, Monika and Josef Naray, who just keep shaking their heads and watching me, sometimes with concern and sometimes with amusement, when I am once again reaching for unicorns and rainbows to make this world a better place.

My wonderful, fantastic, unique, and wise children, Kevin, Nicki, and Shalini Asirvadam, who know my quirks and love me anyway. Thank you for giving me the time to complete this book and being excited with me.

And finally, Kishore Asirvadam, the man by my side for the last twenty years, who saw me happy, sad, excited, angry, hormonal, searching, lost, busy, lazy, and just stood by me and let me be. Thanks for your patience. Thanks for cooking when I didn't find the time. Thanks for being there. Thanks for putting up with me. And thanks for not stopping me from pursuing all my dreams. You are amazing!

Foreword

We cannot solve our problems with the same thinking we used when we created them.

~ Albert Einstein

The signs and symptoms our bodies display are more than physical expressions, instead these manifestations often tell of underlying problems. For example, just as the yellowing of eyes indicate a likely liver disorder, so does an emotional outburst of anger. A woman presenting with PMS symptoms of breast tenderness, irritably and uncontrollable crying the week prior to the start of her menstrual cycle, are also indications of liver dysfunction. Health is more than removal of symptoms; rather it is the ability to maintain homeostasis, also termed as balance, in the face of positive and negative stressors.

Again, health is more than the absence of symptoms. True wellness incorporates the entire being: physical, emotional, mental, spiritual, financial, relational, etc. No health status is devoid of the influence of the environment. Whether extrinsic or intrinsic, the factors of life constantly shape wellbeing.

In Naturopathic and Traditional Chinese medicines, we are taught to utilize a patient's physical symptoms and lab tests, in addition to focusing on the entire person. For example, an individual who constantly has negative thoughts and poor self-talk can be just as detrimental to their health, physically and mentally, as having uncontrolled blood sugar levels is to the physical body.

A quick review of the tenets of various traditional medicines, such as, Traditional Chinese Medicine, Ayurveda, Naturopathic, etc. will explicitly demonstrate the role that physical, emotional, mental and spiritual health play on overall well-being. Thankfully, Alexandra Asirvadam has stretched beyond traditional counseling methods, and has adopted a holistic perspective to mental wellness.

Alexandra causes us to look beyond the physical planes and focus on the entirety of our being. Her passion exudes throughout <u>Balanced Bodies</u>, as she challenges us to look beyond the physical and conventional standards of health care.

She clearly recognizes that by making necessary lifestyle choices, we can change our overall health. Alexandra first identifies the problem(s), educates and then provides succinct overviews and plans, at the end of each chapter to encourage each of us to make the best choices. Not only does she focus on adults, but she also provides tools for the improvement of our children's health.

For anyone who even slightly knows Alexandra, you know that her heart swells to the size of Texas for the betterment of children. Therefore, it is not surprising how Alexandra expertly incorporates tips for supporting your kids' wellbeing throughout the book as well.

Upon initially meeting Alexandra and her daughter in person, their palpable love filled the room. There was no denying the great affection and adoration they felt towards one another. Seeing firsthand this mother's desire to provide the best holistic and comprehensive care for her own children, it is no surprise that her nurturing theme courses throughout this work. We can be thankful for the author's determination that led to the production of an informative, yet relatable, book that allows us to share in her educational spoils.

Thank you, Alexandra, for giving us something more than the typical diet to follow. Instead you present workable plans for all four health levels to promote self-awareness and self-care that can be implemented by all. I know that upon reading <u>Balanced Bodies</u>, you will be equipped with the knowledge needed to accomplish the suggested action plans to become a healthier you: physically, emotionally, mentally, and spiritually.

Blake Gordon, ND, LAc
Naturopathic Doctor, Licensed Acupuncturist
Director of Road Maps 2 Health in Dallas, TX

Introduction

When I heard about three teen suicides within one month in the Canadian town of Saskatoon, Saskatchewan, in June 2017, I started thinking about what makes such young people so desperate that they can't find hope for a good and promising life but rather want to end it. What are the factors that contribute to their pain? What could have been done to prevent those tragedies? Is it simply a mental health issue? Is it a social problem? Is it trouble at school? Is it home life? Is it parenting? Is it something they eat? While this last question sounds somewhat ironic, it really is everything but that. What we eat can affect our emotional and mental health; so can interactions with peers, trouble at home, and lack of parenting. There is usually not just one culprit we can single out. It is many, if not all factors combined, that make the barrel overflow and that lead to such acts of hopelessness and horror.

Even if the main reason why someone would want to end their life is a chemical imbalance in their brain that results in mental health issues, why is this seemingly so much more prevalent these days than it used to be? What has changed in the last few decades that mental health issues seem to be on the rise? Much has changed:

- Increasing pollution
- Deteriorating nutrition
- Worsened drug habits due to easier access

> Constant stress at school and work due to heightened pressure to perform
> Widespread impact of media and social networks that thrives on negativity

Things are obviously changing in our Western world, and our physical and mental health is suffering. We need some guidelines to make the best of our lives despite all the global changes around us that we seemingly cannot do anything about. We need tools that help us to be healthier, happier, more hopeful, and whole in our daily lives.

Today, an ever-increasing number of doctors and experts are exploring how our physical health affects our mental health. Simple and practical suggestions to improve our general well-being, based on their studies and observations, are needed to offer comprehensive and effective help that goes far beyond conventional psychotherapy.

Helping others to help themselves has always been my passion. This goes back to preschool when I chose to be friends with kids that other kids made fun of. I wanted them to be happy and feel included, so I would hang out with them because I was liked and had no problems with anyone. When I was nine, I was in a hospital for major surgery, and a lady in her 50s was brought in for surgery as well. She was terrified of what was going to come. I stepped up to her and told her, matter-of-factly, how this wouldn't be an issue. She would be put to sleep, and when she woke up, it would be over. She might be uncomfortable, but that would be manageable. I was just a little girl but I gave her so much courage that she calmed down for her surgery and didn't worry much anymore. I remember her coming to visit me a few months afterwards to thank me for how much I had helped her, when it should have been the other way around.

Then the tables turned, and I was the one who needed help, psychological help for that matter. I needed to learn how to deal with the physical trauma that would continue to occur over the next 11 years. It had to do with painful medical interventions that at times seemed to be more like experiments and physical torture than healing procedures. But I didn't get the help I needed because nobody knew how much everything I was going through truly affected me; nobody even knew what was exactly done to me behind closed doors, since I decided to keep it to myself to save my parents the pain of knowing. It is ironic that the surgery at age nine, when I helped that lady to get through her ordeal, was the starting point of my over two and a half decades long downward spiral to rock bottom, that led me through physical, emotional, mental, and spiritual pain beyond words. At times, I would go to the extremes: I went back and forth between binge eating and starving myself to keep my weight where I wanted it. Relationships were characterized by my dependency on the other person, and my entire self-worth was based on the man I was with at that moment. I dared not ask for anything that I wanted for myself, fearing they would walk out on me if I did. Friendships consisted mostly of going out, drinking, having fun, and looking for attention from guys, when what I really needed was someone to see my pain and help me to get through it. I experienced outbursts of rage, bouts of depression, and feelings of extreme loneliness. I had no idea what to do with myself. I wavered from procrastination and hours of watching senseless TV, to studying all night long and taking exams without any sleep, being a full-time student with two jobs on the side. There were years of wanting to just be done with life, thereby hurting my soul over and over again, even though I never had any intention of actively harming myself. I experienced mood swings based on unknown triggers that made me go from happy to yelling, crying, and wanting everything to end. I felt out of control, unhappy, unimportant, and entirely useless. And nobody knew the depth of my agony and dysfunction.

Despite these huge struggles in my life, I would still manage to help others through tough times - relationship issues, school issues, family issues, or whatever they approached me with. Most people around me had no clue that I went through this internal turmoil because I had learned to protect others from my pain in my early teenage years, at age 12 to be exact. I even remember the moment when I chose to keep my pain locked up inside for good. I could help others, but I just could not help myself; I did not even realize that I had issues that needed to be resolved, while I met all criteria for posttraumatic stress disorder in the book. What I was living through, though, was MY "normal". Looking back, I see vast dysfunction. Years of medical interventions, trials, failures, and no professional emotional or mental support made me the victim. But I needed to become a survivor and finally start living my life apart from the intense trauma that had shaped me in my core so early on in my life.

From being the one who needed help to becoming the one who helps

My natural tendency to help others coupled with my first-hand experience of trauma and the ensuing dysfunction, as well as my journey out of my personal chaos, led me to my career as licensed professional mental health counselor focusing on trauma, depression, and anxiety. I have become widely open-minded and embrace people's views and perspectives as they come. I accept their struggles and help them to find their truth and ways to accomplish their personal goals, even if their choices are not those that I would make myself. There is no judgment. I have no right to tell anyone how they need to live their lives. There is no way to determine which values are right and which ones are wrong. I also have no right to tell anyone what they have to believe in, spiritually or religiously.

My clients seem to be guided to my private practice and they respond wonderfully to my approach. I can help them to put their feet back on the ground again and learn how to walk. Some are not ready or may not choose to open their minds to the degree that they can work on their most personal matters with someone who may not have their background, their truths, or their religious convictions; someone different from them. To be honest, these are the minority. What most of my clients have mentioned was that they had seen other counselors before, some of them even several, but that I was different from them. Few made them feel so understood. But what am I doing differently? I listen to clients, hear them, accept their truth; I do not try to fix them, nor judge them. I do not tell them what they "should" do, I allow their feelings to matter, I allow them to be different, and I teach them how to not be scared to be different in the first place. I am authentic, honest, and direct, and I give them skills to practice at home every day from the very first session on. I show clients how to work on their thoughts, their anxiety, their communication skills, and their happiness. To me, all these things together are necessary to counsel clients. I am involved in their healing process as if I had to heal myself. My personal goal for my practice is to give my clients tools and let them move on without me as soon as they are ready, rather than keeping them on for months and months.

A slightly different approach to counseling

I use an approach to counseling that incorporates four levels of our being, our physical, emotional, mental, and spiritual bodies, based on Eastern perspectives of healing and spirituality. In fact, there are even higher spiritual bodies on top of these four, but that goes beyond what I can focus on in my counseling practice.

To enhance my knowledge in physical health and nutrition and to be able to educate my clients and give them basic information on how to live healthier, I decided to become a holistic health coach as well. I gained increasing understanding of how much the food we eat every day affects our mental health. I was honestly shocked upon the realization of how unhealthy the food we eat really is. It is demoralizing to think that counselors are trying to help clients to improve their mental health without also addressing their unhealthy eating habits and lack of physical self-care.

While I am not a registered dietitian, nutritionist, or doctor and thus not working with my clients on counting calories and meal plans the way they would, I educate them on how certain foods and deficiencies affect our mental health. I discuss with them what healthier choices could look like, such as fresh instead of processed foods, water instead of sodas, and fruits and vegetables instead of fast foods. It is troubling how many people today not only struggle with making these simple choices, as obvious as they may seem, but also with making them on a consistent basis.

What I want this book to be

This is a book about a holistic and practical approach to mental health. I want to create more awareness of how nutrition and lack of self-care affect mental health. I also want to share simple coping skills and ways to improve our everyday lives, all of which will establish more balance and lead to increased happiness if applied consistently and made a habit, rather than being looked upon as one more chore on our already overflowing schedules. Counseling needs to be more effective, and this can only happen if the whole person is being taken into consideration. As mentioned above, the foundation of my book follows an Eastern concept that describes four levels of our body: physical, emotional, mental, and spiritual. This means that we need to be physically healthy in order to be able to heal our minds, emotionally and mentally. At the same time, we need to bring joy into our lives in order to enhance our emotional health. We also need to work on our mental health in order to allow our physical self-care to show positive effects and be able to feel the joy. Spiritually, we need to find what spiritual or religious beliefs resonate within us most and make us feel alive rather than following doctrines that are imposed on us but do not reach to the depths of our souls.

Traditional counseling focuses on a trusting relationship with the therapist, changing thought processes, exploring beliefs, and how these beliefs affect how clients feel. Some theories stress the importance of solid communication and social interaction, but the physical and spiritual aspects appear to be utterly ignored. The importance of eating healthy and taking care of our physical bodies seems to be obvious once we allow ourselves to think about it, but in fact it is widely neglected and not understood by the majority of clients who enter my practice. The ignorance behind what we are doing to our bodies reveals itself daily in our food choices and the emotional and mental struggles that we experience and endure, rather than addressing them by making much needed changes in our lives.

In my practice, I have observed over and over again how closely physical, emotional, mental, and spiritual aspects are linked. If people are always sad, anxious, or angry, they will develop physical symptoms, such as stomach issues, nausea, aches, and pains. They will think progressively negative thoughts and lose their faith. If people have negative thoughts and find things to criticize all the time, they will not be happy, they will feel uncomfortable in their bodies, and possibly get sick more often, and they might lose their faith as well. If people have no faith, they often do not have positive thoughts, hopes, and dreams like others have who feel connected to their God, Higher Power, or Source; they will not be as happy and positive, and it will affect them physically as well. If people are physically sick, their mood, thoughts, and faith are naturally also affected. All four bodies clearly interact with each other. Therefore, a holistic approach seems to be all-important to become a healthy, happy, and balanced person.

That said, this book offers an approach to mental health counseling that focuses on the whole person. It explores the concept of our four bodies and discusses how the food that we eat affects our brain physically, emotionally, and mentally. It identifies ways to establish balance in our lives, suggesting easy and manageable self-care skills on all four levels. Parenting within this frame of holistic health will be explored to offer simple suggestions for parents of children with mental health challenges. Finally, it includes a practical step-by-step self-care program that can be easily followed, no matter where you are with regard to self-care at this given point in time.

The nutritional information found in here is merely meant to show the interconnection between body and brain, rather than being a complete account of biological processes in the body. The information is based on the work of various experts as stated in footnotes and resources. For more detailed nutritional guidelines or if you want to change your diet, please refer to a registered dietitian, functional medicine doctor, chiropractor, or naturopath.

This book can be of value not only for individuals striving to adopt a healthier lifestyle and learn to manage their personal challenges to find more happiness in life, but also for professionals of various disciplines. A holistic approach to achieve health and well-being is being advocated to offer more comprehensive treatments and support with greater and lasting results.

In a nutshell, my goal for this book is to educate readers on the importance of making healthier food choices, practicing more self-care, finding joy in daily life, pampering themselves a little more, controlling their thoughts consistently, finding relaxation on a regular basis, learning to communicate appropriately, and developing a spiritual or religious practice that works for them. It is a combination of self-care skills on all four levels of the body that will make a difference. Changing only one thing while continuing a number of unhealthy habits will not suffice because one level affects the other. Clearly, balance is the key to a happy and healthy life.

CHAPTER 1

Moving mental health counseling to the next level

The traditional approach to mental health counseling is all about the relationship. Counselors need clients to trust them. In order to establish trust, they listen without judgment, they validate, they reflect, and they encourage. Counselors respect their clients, they are genuine, and they convey a sense of understanding of their clients' struggles. Most approaches focus on the here and now; only a few deal with the past as a starting point of mental health problems. With some approaches, counselors make interpretations and are more directive. With others, clients figure their situation out on their own through the professional relationship with the counselor. Some focus on thought processes, some on behavior modification, and others on relationships and social and family dynamics. Corey (2005) uses the following terms, among others, in his well-known textbook *Theory and Practice of Counseling & Psychotherapy* to describe what various counseling models focus on: thinking, beliefs, behavior, strengths, learning, choices, goals, awareness, responsibility, experience, solutions, impulse, growth, control, meaning, self-determination, truth, integration, communication, human interactions, oppression, relationships, and family. Every single concept Corey mentions has to do with our emotional and mental well-being. And all of these are wonderful things to work on for that perfect life everyone is hoping for. But terms like health, love, happiness, joy, appreciation, gratitude, contentment, balance, and lifestyle seem to be missing from this list. Anyone who has ever tried to improve their life knows that we need to achieve these first before we can work on our greater goals and self-individualization. All these concepts, however, are not only linked to our emotional and mental well-being, but also to our physical health and spirituality.

Spirituality is only mentioned briefly towards the end of Corey's book, where he states, "the field of counseling and psychotherapy has been slow to recognize the need to address spiritual/religious concerns" (466) despite growing evidence that "spiritual values and behaviors can promote physical and psychological well-being" (466). He encourages that counselors also address spiritual and religious issues in counseling. However, traditional counseling programs usually do not offer any training in this field.

The importance of addressing physical health and its effects on mental health in a counseling setting is not mentioned at all in Corey's book, let alone in any of the current models of psychotherapy. Counselors get no training in even the most basic concepts of physical health unless they pursue an additional certification or degree. This absolutely needs to be part of their curriculum in order to assist others in achieving a healthy well-being, emotionally, mentally, and physically. We can no longer ignore the importance of strengthening the body through nutrition and physical exercise when pursuing emotional and mental healing.

There have been numerous discussions regarding the dualism of body and mind according to Western health perspectives. They are treated separately in the West, when these two realms, according to Eastern health perspectives, are connected and communicate with each other constantly. If health care tended more towards holism, the way of diagnosing and treating disorders by merely looking at symptoms could not be upheld. It neglects to look for underlying causes of the symptoms expressed by body and brain. Holistic approaches such as functional medicine look for underlying causes of physical and psychological issues and aim to heal the body at the cell level, rather than treating mere symptoms. According to functional medicine, as noted by Dr. Martha Herbert in her introduction to Dr. Mark Hyman's book *The Ultra Mind Solution*, problems in the body lead to problems in the brain, and chemical imbalances in mental disorders are a metabolic problem and can be treated on a bodily level. Hyman even believes that only 10% of individuals with mental health challenges are nutritionally, metabolically, and biochemically balanced enough to fully benefit from psychotherapy. He states that physical balance needs to be established first before therapy can even begin (13).

There are also wellness models which suggest strength-based strategies that are applied for physical, intellectual, social, occupational, emotional, and spiritual development to reach our potential, establish balance in life, and find our meaning and purpose within our environment. These models specifically focus on:

- Family, friends, relationships, and community
- Education, work, and stress management
- Love, spirituality, and identity
- Nutrition and exercise
- Self-care, emotional wellness, and expression of feelings
- Environment and culture[1]

The interconnection of these categories seems obvious. Making individualized choices in all these categories consistently will bring us closer to optimal living, but can also be a challenge, especially when people feel alone and have no social support. Loneliness may lead to lack of exercise, alcohol use, and lack of sleep, resulting in fatigue, life dissatisfaction, suicidal behavior, and increased feeling of stress in life. Wellness can be impacted by perceived stress, as well as feelings of revenge, lack of self-acceptance, lack of a sense of belonging, and any kind of discrimination. A good network of friends and family together with skills to cope with demanding situations and stress are key for psychological well-being. Wellness models appear to be a step ahead of counseling theory in terms of their holistic approach, focusing on body, mind, and spirit.

While counseling is merely focusing on emotions, thought processes, behavior, and social life, functional medicine makes it clear that our brain is directly affected by our physical health and nutrition. Wellness models have already incorporated this concept which shows the importance to also broaden the counseling approach, since trying to improve how our brain works appears pointless when we limit its functionality with the food we eat every day. The following chapters will put light on how nutritional deficiencies can impact our brain, thus negatively affecting counseling progress if physical health keeps being ignored.

CHAPTER 2

The four bodies

The concept of the four bodies is really a fairly simple one. It entails that our body is not just our physical being or what we see. Our bodies are surrounded by energy, some call it an aura, that some people claim to be able to sense. What many don't know is that most of us can feel the energy around us. Just imagine walking past people who are always thinking negative thoughts and who are mean-spirited. Many would say it feels uncomfortable being around them, and they don't want to be anywhere near. That means they are picking up on their negative energy that brings other people down. What is this negative energy though?

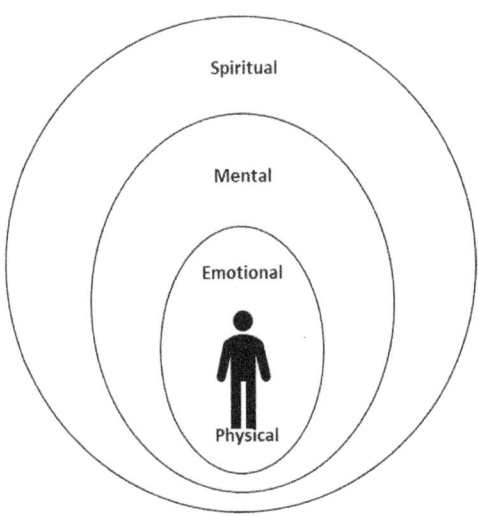

The physical body

While only the physical body appears to be tangible, the other three bodies are in fact clearly perceptible to us as far as our well-being is concerned. Physically, we can easily pinpoint aches and pains and aim to heal the source of our ailments or, which is less optimal, mask our symptoms with painkillers. We can take care of our physical body from inside and outside in the form of a healthy diet, exercise, massage, hygiene, and so on. A healthy body allows us to partake actively in life and projects, as we choose, and can make us feel strong and healthy.

The emotional body

The emotional body surrounds the physical body. This is where our feelings are located. When we are happy and excited, we attract others with our bubbly energy that may even be contagious. When we are sad, we will find that others will be more considerate and caring around us to support us, because they can feel that we are struggling. If we are constantly in a depressed mood and low, we will probably end up pushing away other people, not just with our behavior but also with our energy because the energy of depression is draining to everyone else around us, just like it is for us when we experience it firsthand.

When experiencing emotional pain, we are very aware of it, but we can have a tough time making others understand where it comes from if it does not pertain to obvious causes like grief or loss of some kind. Emotional pain is real to the individual suffering from it, but difficult to understand for everyone else. It is also not as easy to take care of our emotional body because most have no idea how to go about it. Working on our relationships and stress in life will impact our emotional health greatly. A healthy emotional body allows us to enjoy life and experience happiness most days.

The mental body

Outside of the emotional body is another layer of energy, our mental body. This is the energy of our thoughts and minds. Depending on whether we are positive or negative, hopeful or hopeless, motivated or stuck, adventurous or procrastinating, our energy will emanate accordingly, and it will also be picked up on by people around us. Some people are so easy to talk to because they are open-minded and embracing while others seem to be looking for confrontation and conflict constantly. It is easy to see then why we would rather be around positive people than negative ones. Just like with the low energy of depression, the energy of negative people is similarly draining.

It becomes obvious why individuals with mental health challenges experience such devastating isolation. It is a combination of not having the energy and strength to pull themselves out of their personal darkness along with the ignorance of people who simply do not understand what is going on within them. In addition, they often run into judgment because there is still a stigma about having mental health issues. Their resulting helplessness leads to avoidance, and low energies cause strain on loved ones resulting in disconnected relationships.

There are energy healing techniques that directly deal with these energies of depression, pain, and substance abuse. Practitioners report that when they get in contact with them, it hurts them physically. This observation also validates the pain that people affected by mental health issues live with every day.

Suffering from mental pain can be torture for the person affected by it, and there is no doubt that what they feel is real to them. Like emotional pain, it is not obvious how to soothe mental pain or how to do mental self-care to prevent problems in the first place. The mental body is greatly impacted by our thought processes, and learning to control them will help us ease some of the pain we feel. A healthy mental body allows us to think clearly, see things for what they are, move towards our goals, and simply have peace of mind.

The spiritual body

The physical, emotional, and mental bodies are surrounded by the spiritual body, our faith, our spirituality, our connection to God, our Higher Power, our Source, Universe, or simply Nature. The thought of us being embedded in spiritual energy and surrounded and protected by who or what we believe in, is a beautiful one. A strong sense of spirituality can facilitate healing on all levels, physical, emotional, and mental. The person who enters a room and seemingly makes the lights come on is most likely well balanced in their physical, emotional, and mental self-care and in addition to that, spiritually well connected. However, the problem is that a continuous struggle on any of these levels can result in a lack of faith. Losing our faith usually becomes noticeable by others because it leads to a lack of direction, a lack of meaning, a lack of deeper relationships, and a lack of motivation to strive higher.

Some people live and breathe their faith; they feel it inside and out. They feel the strength they gain from it and feel the hole if it is missing. Trust, hope, and a sense of meaning are often based on spirituality, and a healthy spiritual body allows for unconditional love and a clear direction in life. When talking about the four bodies, they may not be there for us to see or touch, but they can be felt clearly and without any doubt.

Establishing balance between the four bodies

Basically, our four bodies describe who we are. We are not just our physical selves; our emotions, thoughts, and beliefs define us as a person. If you will, the four bodies describe our personalities, and balancing them means to become a more balanced and whole person in our daily lives.

Throughout the next chapters links and associations will become obvious and how tied-in these four levels are with each other. A change on one level will affect each of the others. It proves to be very difficult to separate the following discussion into four categories and not repeat the same information in all four chapters.

In the discussion of the physical body, the effects of nutrition and exercise on mood, focus, and spirituality cannot be ignored. The chapter on the emotional body mainly focuses on which food choices affect our mood, but also on relationships and several types of stress. The chapter on the mental body goes more into detail how specific nutrients affect our neurotransmitters in the brain, since brain health is key to be able to benefit most from psychotherapy. The importance of a healthy lifestyle and controlled thought processes for our mental health are also being addressed. Next, thoughts on spirituality are being discussed that complement the foregoing chapters. And finally, step by step suggestions to put a self-care plan into action are being offered. However, it needs to be understood that no coping skills taught in therapy can make up for lack of physical health. If physical health is what causes psychological symptoms, the root of the problem is clearly missed with traditional psychotherapy that fails to address nutrition and exercise.

The importance of a balanced life can be seen in the following illustration. If our core is filled with healthy behaviors, feelings, thoughts, and beliefs we can experience a whole and happy life. Our core can make us stronger against any outside stressors and temptations to let ourselves withdraw into a deep dark hole in the face of adversities.

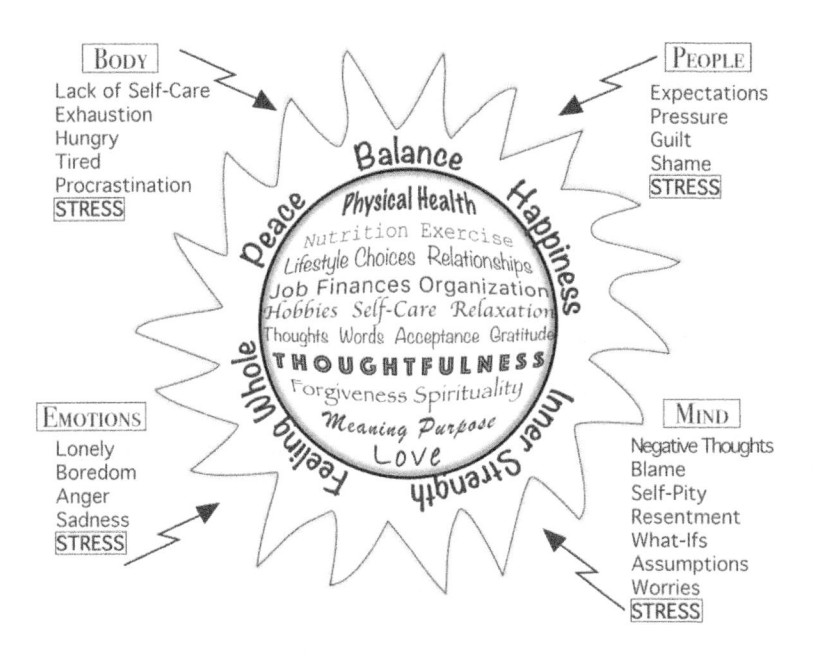

Body
Lack of Self-Care
Exhaustion
Hungry
Tired
Procrastination
STRESS

People
Expectations
Pressure
Guilt
Shame
STRESS

Balance
Physical Health
Nutrition Exercise
Lifestyle Choices Relationships
Job Finances Organization
Hobbies Self-Care Relaxation
Thoughts Words Acceptance Gratitude
THOUGHTFULNESS
Forgiveness Spirituality
Meaning Purpose
Love

Peace · Happiness · Inner Strength · Feeling Whole

Emotions
Lonely
Boredom
Anger
Sadness
STRESS

Mind
Negative Thoughts
Blame
Self-Pity
Resentment
What-Ifs
Assumptions
Worries
STRESS

CHAPTER 3

The physical body

In our Western society, healing is approached differently than in Eastern countries. When we have pain, we cover it. When we are ill, we treat the symptoms. We have pills to manage diabetes, high cholesterol, heart disease, blood pressure, allergies, and pain, but we often don't address the cause of these diseases. According to Harvard's Dr. Lucian Leape, the leading causes of death are now heart disease, cancer, and diabetes, followed by car accidents and iatrogenic diseases, which are accidental deaths caused by medical errors in hospitals and by the pharmaceutical industry. The following numbers show the recent increase in physical health problems:

Diabetes tripled since 1980, even diabetes in children has increased by 30%. According to Dr. Mark Hyman, a physician and New York Times best-selling author, one in four teenage boys had prediabetes or diabetes in 2008 as compared to one in ten in 2000. 50 million Americans have thyroid or autoimmune diseases. 60 million Americans are affected by allergies, 15 million of which specifically by food allergies. According to Dr. Robin Berzin, a functional medicine doctor, the number of children with food allergies has gone up by 50% between 1977 and 2011. According to Gary Taubes, author of *The Case Against Sugar*, obesity increased by 250% over the last 50 years. 70% of Americans and 40% of American children are overweight. $70 billion are spent on weight loss every year. 75% of healthcare money is spent on preventable lifestyle diseases.

These numbers are high and concerning, and you might wonder what is causing this huge increase. Whatever we put into our bodies has clearly an effect on how our bodies are holding up. 90% of the consumed food is supermarket food that is mostly processed. 100 million people eat fast food. Processed foods, unhealthy fats, sugar, artificial colors and flavors can clearly influence physical and mental health. Nutrition affects our feelings and thought processes and our body cannot function when proper nutrients are lacking[1]. 70-80% of processed foods contain genetically modified organisms. The debate whether GMOs are harmful or not continues. The food industry claims they are harmless, however, there are various organizations that claim otherwise and assure that GMOs cause all kinds of physical and/or mental problems in animal studies and humans alike. This book is not the place to dive into this debate, but the stance taken here is simple: We cannot create things better than nature itself, so why change them? Food is grown by nature to sustain life, so let's stick to natural foods rather than those produced in laboratories, and let nature take care of us rather than money driven industries.

Exposure to hormones, antibiotics, and chemicals like artificial sweeteners, MSG, and pesticides in our food early on in life have been linked to autism, neurobehavioral problems in children, and hyperactivity. Changes in mood, aggressive behavior, attention difficulties, sleep problems, lower intellectual performance, and memory loss have been observed. Cases of autism, mood disorders, and ADHD have increased drastically over the last 30 years[2].

Along with the food we put into our bodies, we also ingest toxins from recreational drugs, alcohol, and pollution through our respiratory system, digestion, and skin. Pollution is everywhere, in the air we breathe and the water we drink. Toxic chemicals are found everywhere these days, as well, and we ingest them daily. They can affect our body, brain, and nervous system. Our bodies are constantly fighting substances they do not know what to do with. Toxicity has become a huge issue and results from herbicides, pesticides, metals in our foods, medication, silver dental fillings, water supply and soil, additives and chemicals in our food itself and immediate environment. Pesticides can be found in 80% of foods. There are indications that electromagnetic fields from cell phones, computers, TVs, microwaves, and other electronics alter our cellular metabolism and generate free radicals which are toxic to the brain and lead to memory loss, dementia, Alzheimer's, and mood disorders[3]. As healthy as we try to be, it proves to be very difficult to live an exclusively clean life. Therefore, doing the best we can to stay natural and keeping it simple regarding food choices, cleaning supplies, hygiene, and "lifestyle choices" is essential in our highly industrial society.

Ann Cooper, an internationally recognized author, chef, educator, and public speaker, propagates to change the way we feed our children. Based on their nutrition, childhood obesity has tripled over the last 25 years, 50% are expected to have cancer in their lifetime, there is a 300% increase in asthma, a 400 % increase in allergies and ADHD, and a 1500% increase in autism. Cooper blames chemicals in our food that we feed our children, as well as the amounts of sugar, for these incredible numbers. She also states that one out of three Caucasians and one out of two African Americans and Hispanics born after 2000 are expected to develop diabetes in their lifetime. This is also the first generation that is believed to have a shorter life expectancy than their parents.

Dr. Christiane Northrup, a leading authority in the field of women's health and wellness, states that 42% of 1st-3rd grade girls want to be thinner and 81% of 10-year olds are afraid of getting fat, an emotional and mental aspect which is bound to affect the way these children eat in the present and future. This pressure from societal norms may impact their relationship with food and may start a long road of diets that will not work, rather than learning how to live a healthy and full life and how to choose proper food to nourish their bodies.

Jacka (2017) established that healthy diets, based on nutrient-dense, plant-based foods and quality sources of protein, are clearly associated with fewer mental health issues in children and adolescents. On the other hand, unhealthy diets with higher intake of processed, sugary, and fatty foods, are associated with increased mental health problems, independent of key environmental factors and consistently across countries, cultures, and age groups.

The bottom line, according to Dr. David Katz, an internist and preventive medicine specialist, is that nonsmokers who have a good diet, regular exercise, and control their weight have an 80% lesser likelihood of developing any chronic disease. If you incorporate only one of these factors in your life, you already reduce your risk by 50%. A Danish twin study showed that only 20% of life expectancy is dictated by genes, while 80% is dictated by lifestyle and environment. These numbers indicate that we could have great control over our health and well-being, if we only adjusted our lifestyle accordingly. If we focused on our self-care daily in the same way we sleep and breathe, we would not only feel much better physically, we would also decrease our prescription medication intake and doctor visits which will save us time and money, resulting in less stress, clearer minds, and increased happiness. This leaves you wondering why it seems so hard to find the time and energy to dedicate a certain amount of time every day to taking care of our precious bodies that we directly depend on.

Dr. Mark Hyman suggests focusing on nutrition, hormones, inflammation, digestion, detoxification, energy, and calming the mind in order to address physical imbalances that show up in the brain. Covering up the symptoms, as it is done in Western medicine, cannot heal but only harm the body even more. Acid-blocking drugs used for heartburn are a simple but perfect example: they may take care of the symptom at hand, but they are essentially harmful for the body because they also prevent mineral absorption[4].

Men are less likely to follow healthy eating recommendations. They eat less fruits and vegetables, more saturated fats, drink more sodas, and make easy, but not always healthy, lifestyle choices they feel don't need to be changed because they do not notice any direct negative consequences. Married couples, on the other hand, tend to eat healthier than unmarried individuals[5], indicating that with support and shared goals better choices can be made more easily.

Lifestyle choices

Lifestyle, apart from nutrition, also comes along with a number of unhealthy choices that we consider "living the way I want to", rather than conforming to societal norms. Recreational drug use, alcohol use, and nicotine have been around for a very long time. However, modern drugs are especially unpredictable because they are chemical compounds that have not existed before. They obviously affect our brains, some more, some less. Some can trigger mental illness, especially when individuals have a predisposition already; and some can be even lethal.

Nicotine has been linked to depression. It constricts the blood flow to the brain and is toxic, making regular use harmful. Four or more alcoholic drinks a day double the risk of dementia, while small amounts seem to decrease that risk. Alcohol and caffeine are major contributors to a depressed and unstable mood, anxiety, and sleep problems[6], which is a perfect illustration of how the physical, emotional, mental, and spiritual bodies are intertwined with poor choices that harm our body and consequently can lead to emotional and mental problems that in turn will reinforce the negative behavior as a coping skill; and the downward spiral begins.

Alcohol is highly addictive, and alcohol addiction is incredibly destructive. It tends to sneak up on you with parties and a "good ole time", leading to the habitual six pack or bottle of wine, until people start losing loved ones, jobs, and things they have worked for. The body cannot digest alcohol, it is not made to process it. Alcohol is basically poison for us and slows down the brain metabolism. It is a depressant, and while at first it seems to up one's mood, it gradually depresses it to the point that the illusion of self-medication keeps the addiction going. It depletes B vitamins which affects our mood. Any substance that is so harmful cannot possibly be a justifiable solution to make us feel better when things do not go the way we want them to. That said, alcohol use does not go hand in hand with a healthy lifestyle and nutrition, and neither does it with physical, emotional, mental, and spiritual balance.

Marijuana seems to be harmless to most, but it affects the part of the brain that is linked to schizophrenia and can trigger temporary or permanent delusions and hallucinations. It also can be found laced with other drugs without the knowledge of the consumer, and it is unclear how many chemicals this popular recreational drug contains. All the side effects of smoking tobacco can be found with marijuana as well. It is a mind-altering drug that people get used to, and it affects mood, behavior, attitude, and choices. As far as other drugs are concerned, most will agree their damaging and destructive qualities can severely hurt our bodies and brains indefinitely.

Another concern is the prescription of pharmaceuticals to mask symptoms of disease, which happens incredibly freely these days and is the Western approach to medicine. Medications frequently have side effects, and warnings on the labels tell us how many systems in the body one single medication can impact negatively. Often medications are prescribed to treat the symptoms of side effects of other medications. Most medications are prescribed to help with lifestyle diseases, resulting in people taking medication for high cholesterol, high blood pressure, diabetes, etc., basically allowing people to continue to make their unhealthy choices at the same time, which seems entirely senseless and self-defeating.

Many medications deplete our minerals and vitamins, leading to other health issues. Coenzyme Q10 for example, which makes energy for our cells, is shut down by cholesterol-lowering statins, beta-blockers, and antidiabetic drugs[7]. Vitamin B, which is crucial for our cognitive functions and mood, is being depleted by acid-blocking medication, aspirin, estrogens, diuretics, seizure medication, and anti-inflammatory drugs including ibuprofen. Acid-blocking medication prevents protein digestion, which impacts our neurotransmitters, resulting in mood, attention, and memory issues. It also affects the absorption of magnesium, which may lead to anxiety and mood disorders. Acetaminophen depletes Glutathione, potentially also leading to mental and physical health issues[8]. These are just a few examples to illustrate how commonly prescribed medications and over-the-counter medication can contribute to mental health issues without anyone possibly suspecting such side effects.

Dr. Daniel Amen is a psychiatrist who explored mental health issues and how the brain works. He has performed thousands of brain scans in order to be able to see whether there is a physical component to mental health. He managed to identify probable causes like brain trauma, injuries, over-activity, or under-activity, and helped many patients to literally heal their brains. Examples of Amen's findings are that brain trauma and injuries can lead to aggressive behavior, over-activity of certain parts of the brain can lead to inflexible negative thought processes and agitation, while under-activity of parts of the brain can lead to lack of concentration and conflict-seeking behaviors[9]. Being able to go to the source of the problem makes clinical interventions much more straightforward and effective, compared to the hit-and-miss approach of traditional psychiatry. Amen found that brains are highly sensitive, can be injured easily, but can also heal. As he points out, all the following are harmful to our brains:

- Drugs and too much alcohol
- Infections, obesity, and sleep apnea
- Hypertension and elevated blood pressure on the top end of the normal range
- Diabetes and blood sugar that is high but still considered in the normal range
- Traumatic head injuries
- Many medications
- Bad diet and processed foods
- Sugar, sweeteners, and artificial colors
- Environmental toxins and pesticides
- Unbalanced hormone levels
- Chronic stress, negative thinking, and being around unhealthy people[10]

Epigenetics is studying the effect of our lifestyle, such as diet, stress, toxins, drug and alcohol abuse, and certain prescribed medications, on future generations. Drug and alcohol use during pregnancy is known to often have terrible consequences for the fetus. Severe cases can be observed in fetal alcohol syndrome, newborns with intense withdrawal symptoms, lower IQs, behavior issues, and physical damage to body and brain. However, it seems ignorant to claim that there are no effects whatsoever in other cases of drug and alcohol abuse during pregnancy that were lucky enough to not end up so tragically. Unhealthy habits and lifestyles can switch genes on and off and thereby affect who knows how many generations to come. The choices we are making today on a daily basis can clearly have a huge impact on our children and grandchildren. We will have to face the consequences of our behavior, however, so will the people we love most[11].

It remains to be seen how the developments of the last decades regarding food industry, pharmaceutical industry, bioengineering, and chemicals used in our daily lives, as well as drugs, alcohol, and nicotine use, may lead to genetic changes in our bodies and brains. Over the centuries, our bodies have always tried to adjust to environmental changes, but they don't always manage to do so entirely. Some experts claim that this has happened as far as grains are concerned, which many people simply cannot digest properly because they are not part of our traditional diet. What appears to be obvious is that our bodies have to constantly work on overdrive to keep up with all the changes that have been imposed on them over the most recent decades and fight these unfamiliar and, for our bodies, harmful substances every day.

The physical body – *an overview*

- Heart disease, cancer, diabetes, autoimmune diseases, allergies, and obesity are on the rise.
- Medications manage symptoms rather than heal the body.
- Processed foods, sugars, and unhealthy fats affect our physical and mental health.
- Additives in our food have been linked to autism, neurobehavioral problems, hyperactivity, changes in mood, aggressive behavior, attention difficulties, sleep problems, lower intellectual performance, and memory loss.
- Pollution and toxic chemicals affect our body, brain, and nervous system.
- Electromagnetic fields have been linked to memory loss, dementia, Alzheimer's, and mood disorders.
- Pressure from society affects how our children eat.
- A healthy lifestyle includes diet, exercise, self-care, and calming the mind.
- Nicotine has been linked to depression.
- Alcohol has been linked to depression, anxiety, sleep problems, and dementia.
- Caffeine has been linked to depression, anxiety, and sleep problems.
- Any recreational drug affects mood, behavior, attitude, and choices.
- Prescribed medication has side effects and can deplete minerals and vitamins.
- Mental health issues are linked to physical changes in the brain.
- Unhealthy choices and lifestyle lead to lasting changes in our genes.

How to feed your body

We need to feed our bodies properly, there are no two ways about it. And the fast food industry is, as the name says, an industry and has little to do with proper nourishment. Ingredients are bought in bulk and cheap and are part of a money-making business. Fresh and natural foods are best made at home, and this does not necessarily take as much time as people think. Finding a handful of easy and fast recipes to start with is all we need. We can prepare food for two days, so we don't have to cook every day if time is an issue, which for many it is.

We also need to figure out what we can and cannot have, bodies are different, and what works for one may not work for another, just with everything else in life. Not everyone is made to be a vegetarian and not everyone thrives on animal products. In addition to that, our body may change with age, and what works for us at one point in time may not be good for us as we get older. Listening to our body and feeling how it responds to the food we eat is key to adjust to the changes we go through over the years.

The choices we make for breakfast, lunch, dinner, and snacks are critical. How much processed food do we eat, and what is processed food to begin with? Processed food is anything that does not grow in nature in that form. It is as simple as that. When you change what nature provides by adding one ingredient, you process it. This definition turns cooking into food processing as well. When people talk about processed food that is harmful for us, they usually refer to commercially processed food as found in supermarkets. It is full of additives, preservatives, food colorings, and chemicals in order to increase its shelf life. When we cook, we preferably use fresh ingredients rather than ready-made processed sauces and mixes. This does not necessarily add hours to the cooking process when using simple and fast recipes, which can be found online in abundance to make our lives easier. The bottom line is, we may want to avoid any food that has more than five ingredients on its label. We may also want to think twice about eating foods containing ingredients that no regular person could ever pronounce.

Another question to ask ourselves is, how often do we eat fresh foods, as in fruits and vegetables? We need to find ways to incorporate our leafy greens in soups or add them to our meat dish if our kids refuse to eat them as a side dish. There is broccoli, cauliflower, carrots, cabbage, squash, tomatoes, bell pepper, mushrooms, brussel sprouts, okra, beans, lentils, onions, garlic, and much more ready to be consumed as fresh produce that is really good for us. We can find simple dishes that can be prepared in a matter of minutes and make a commitment to ourselves to cook at least a couple vegetable dishes a week. We can eat some fruit or sweet vegetables like carrots to ward off sweet cravings.

What does our breakfast look like? Do we consider it healthy or could we make it healthier? Do we eat ready-made cereals? Do we eat eggs and bacon? Do we eat at all? We can make breakfast definitely more interesting by changing it up. We can always add our fruits and veggies, whatever we choose to have. Fruits with Greek yogurt or kefir, nuts, and seeds instead of cereal boxes may be an alternative. Onions, celery, bell peppers, and mushrooms can be added to scrambled eggs. Avocados and lettuce can go into any sandwich if that is what we choose to have. Leafy greens, fruit, almond or coconut milk, nuts, and seeds can be blended into a smoothie. These are some simple examples for a healthier start into the day. After all, how we start the day determines how the rest of our day is going to turn out in the end.

How often do we eat out for lunch and dinner, and how often do we have home-cooked meals? Fast food places are just too inviting when we are really hungry and tired after a hard day of work. But how about making a big pot of stew or beans that lasts a couple days and can be heated up when coming home? Or for those who despise heating up food, maybe cutting up veggies the day before, so they only need to be thrown into the pot when getting home could be an option. This way the cooking process is much faster than if everything had to be prepared from scratch there and then. When we take our lunch to work and heat it up in order to avoid fast food places, we also know exactly what is in our food and what we are eating. Finding options and giving them a real chance in order to eat a healthy meal is key to lasting physical and mental health. It's about creating new habits and making them as easy as possible.

Another important change for many is what we have for snacks. Most are sugary, processed, or fatty because this way they don't go bad as quickly, come in handy packages, and taste the way we want them to because we got used to this taste years ago. Little packages with olives and raw cheese can be prepared at home instead and taken with us to work. Nuts and seeds can be awesome to snack on. A bowl of guacamole always seems to be a wonderful treat for most. If we like crackers and something crunchy, we can eat these with hummus and add some nutrition that way. And of course, smoothies, fruits, and raw vegetables can also be consumed for a snack at any time.

We need to learn to be honest to ourselves and watch the sugar we eat every day. Reading labels helps with that. 4 grams of sugar are equivalent to 1 teaspoon of sugar. Checking candy, chocolate, crackers, and chips, but also salad dressings, juices and other drinks, sauces, and cereal boxes can be very insightful and frightening at the same time. Most of us are not aware of how much sugar we really consume on a daily basis in addition to the sugar we put in our coffee and tea.

Most of us need to drink more water and learn to live without sodas. Sodas are full of sugar and chemicals and do a lot of harm and no good. For some this is a gradual transformation, while others manage to quit immediately. One small can of soda contains ten teaspoons of sugar, which is more than our daily recommended amount of six teaspoons. A large soda contains triple that amount. What many people don't know is that fruit juices have the same amount of sugar as sodas. Orange juice has even more than that. However, if sugar is replaced in so-called sugar-free drinks, chemicals are usually added instead, which are just as harmful. Dehydration can cause a number of ailments, such as headache, fatigue, and dizziness. It can affect our ability to focus and our general physical well-being. Therefore, avoiding sugary beverages and drinking more water instead is crucial for our health and can often almost miraculously "heal" our daily physical discomforts.

Another critical point to remember is to watch our portion size at all times. We tend to overeat, partially due to getting too hungry or time constraints, and feel miserable afterwards, often needing medication to aid digestion, which, as mentioned before, is a problem of its own. In order to reduce our portion size, we can eat more slowly and chew more. This not only gives our body the chance to send the signal that we had enough at the right time, but we also allow enzymes and digestive juices to break up our food better for a more thorough digestion, avoiding the need for medication in the first place. That said, we may consider not drinking any liquids while we eat to prevent our gastric acid from getting too diluted, which hinders digestion. Drinking water twenty minutes before and/or after dinner seems to be more beneficial for our digestion instead.

When working on improving our diet and changing our habits, we cannot be too strict with ourselves, otherwise we feel guilty or weak if we mess up. Some experts suggest eating healthy ninety percent of the time, and allow for little treats the other ten percent. Others talk about an eighty-twenty ratio. The importance is to keep working on improving our health and diet, no matter if we slip up or not. Every healthy food we add is one more than we ate before and replaces unhealthy foods one at a time.

Food sensitivities

One important step to determine how to adjust our diet is to check for food sensitivities. Naturopaths and functional medicine doctors offer these tests, and they show what our body can and cannot handle. Food sensitivities may not even be overly noticeable at first, but in the long run will most likely lead to systemic inflammation and chronic issues, such as autoimmune diseases and digestion problems. Once food sensitivities are determined or excluded, healthy choices regarding nutrition can be made in a more personalized manner. Until then, eating fresh foods, reducing sugar, and adding water to our diet may go a long way.

If the cost for naturopaths or functional medicine doctors is an issue, we can find out ourselves if we react to certain foods, using the elimination diet. It requires discipline and some time but can be eye opening. At first, typical foods that people tend to be sensitive to are taken out of our diet for two weeks in order to get them out of our system. This includes refined sugar, dairy, gluten, eggs, soy, and corn and basically means major components of the typical Western diet. As a side note, soy and corn are common ingredients in processed foods, and they are mostly genetically modified today, which may contribute to the fact that they seem to trigger food sensitivities or even allergic reactions in a growing number of people. With the elimination diet all these food groups are first removed from our diet and then reintroduced one at a time. While temporarily limiting these foods, we can eat fruits and vegetables, meats, and gluten-free grains such as quinoa, oats, and brown rice. Especially when adjusting our diet, it is important to plan meals ahead of time, so a hungry and desperate brain does not revert back to the fast food place around the corner or whatever else it has been used to.

After two weeks of avoiding typical foods that may cause sensitivities, the body will have detoxed from them. If there are sensitivities to one or more of them, bodily and mental changes can usually be observed, such as improved digestion, less pain, feeling of well-being, less fatigue, increased focus and interests, and a happier mood in general. At that point one of the eliminated food groups can be reintroduced, such as dairy products. Once eaten at least three times over three days without any discomfort and physical or mental deterioration, this food group may be considered safe. If negative symptoms and discomfort return, a food sensitivity has been detected and this food group needs to be removed from our diet again and avoided going forward. Once again cleared from our system, the next food group can be added back into the diet.

In addition to the elimination diet, Korn suggests that a pulse test can help us to detect possible food sensitivities. To do so we need to take our pulse before getting out of bed, one minute before each meal, thirty minutes after each meal, and just before going to bed. The pulse is taken for one minute each time and needs to be recorded for two to three days. Whenever our pulse is elevated more than six to eight beats per minute after any meal, we need to look at what we had to eat and identify the possible source of this increase. We can experiment with the identified foods to see if the increase repeats itself when eating these foods again[24]. If that is the case, avoiding these foods going forward may prevent future ailments of physical and/or mental nature.

Experimenting with different foods is one thing, changing our diet for good is another, especially if we must eliminate entire food groups. When intending to do so, working with a nutritionist or registered dietician to ensure appropriate nutrition is recommended.

How to feed your body – an overview

- Check for processed foods in your diet.
- Find easy and fast recipes to cook your food at home.
- Eat fresh vegetables.
- Eat fresh fruits.
- Make your breakfast healthier and "fresher".
- Take homecooked meals to work for lunch.
- Cook enough for two days or prepare for cooking by cutting up ingredients beforehand.
- Eating out is not only expensive, you also don't know what you get.
- Find healthy snacks without sugar, less salt, and unhealthy fats.
- Read labels.
- Drink more water.
- Check for food sensitivities.
- Be kind to yourself, no matter what.

How to get your body moving

Physical exercise has shown to promote new brain cell formation and improve memory, mood, and cognitive functions of the brain, preventing dementia and benefitting all four levels of the body. It increases the neurotransmitters dopamine, which affects the ability to focus, and serotonin, which has to do with the ability to stay calm and relax. These will be discussed in more detail in a later chapter. Exercise can be very challenging for many people due to time constraints, fatigue, lack of interest, or simply not knowing what kind of exercise could be enjoyable.

Exercise does not have to mean going to the gym five times a week. It can be walking, slowly at first and briskly eventually, through the neighborhood for 15 minutes, or doing a few exercises three times a week before having a shower, before going to bed, or even during your favorite show. It is done more easily in company, because it adds fun and accountability, but exercising alone works just as well.

We can get a DVD if we need instructions or choose from the many videos offered online that suggest an exercise routine. Some personal trainers offer online challenges to follow their exercise routines daily for a certain amount of time. We can change up what kind of exercise we choose at regular intervals to keep things interesting and keep us going.

Others who love to exercise may be involved in sports, join a class, go to the gym on a regular basis, or have a hobby like working towards a half marathon, riding a bike, swimming for speed or endurance, rock climbing, or rowing. As with everything else in life, there is not one right way of doing things – whatever works is great. We just have to make it our own, be fully aware of all the benefits we are getting from it, and stick with it not because we are told to but because we love and need it.

When parents involve their children in exercise, it proves to be motivating for everybody. Riding bikes, practicing for a 5k, hiking, swimming, renting a boat, roller blading, roller skating, ice skating, and rock climbing are all activities that can be done with kids and are fun. While exercise can leave us very tired, it usually improves the mood and provides the feeling of accomplishment.

The crucial point of exercise is to get our heart rate going a couple times during the exercise period. This means if we go for a walk we can run for a minute two or three times during our walk to get our heart rate up. According to some experts, moving our body and periodically increasing our heart rate is the most beneficial type of exercise.

We always need to make sure that the exercise we choose fits our body in terms of health, age, and weight.

The point is not to continuously increase our strength, unless we make this our goal, but to maintain and improve our well-being.

Yoga

Yoga makes the interconnection of the four levels of the body even clearer and is a perfect approach for holistic health if its philosophy is followed in its entirety. Yoga and qigong have shown to have positive effects in terms of being in tune with our body, energy levels, mental clarity, and concentration[12]. Yoga, tai chi, Ayurveda, and Chinese medicine strive to restore balance in our physical body and mind and utilize the body's innate healing systems. Therefore, attention is put on ourselves, as compared to Western healing approaches that simply look for an outside fix. These Eastern techniques are not only of a physical nature, they also have an element of enlightenment, spirituality, and mental and emotional growth.

Yoga psychology identifies five points that lead to dissatisfaction with life: ego and self-centeredness, cravings beyond what we need, resisting something, ignorance, and fear of death[13]. Accepting that not everything in life has to do with us and being happy for others is a challenge for many. In our society we are overly focused on controlling, fixing, and managing, which results in having trouble letting go of any type of control. This makes us self-centered. We are exposed to all the things people can have through media and social media. We focus too much on what we want, rather than on what we have, which brings about a lack of appreciation for our present environment, including people in our lives. That said, we want to learn to savor the moment rather than creating an emptiness by wanting what we do not have. It is very common to, out of fear, resist ideas and changes that we want to make in our lives. What we know is comfortable, what we don't know is perceived as a threat to our stability and safety. However, this mindset holds us captive and stuck, leading to dissatisfaction and unhappiness. Ignorance means not considering other possibilities, not knowing but also not striving to search for the truth, settling for where we are, not wanting to even be confronted with the idea that there might be better paths and possibilities for us to live our life, and keeping ourselves close-minded rather than reaching for insight and enlightenment. Fear of death, fear of our terminality, and fear of losing what we have appears to be rooted in lack of faith that there may be something greater than us that gives our lives meaning. If people are not spiritual by nature, they often do not manage to live in the present moment and simply fear what is going to come because they don't trust themselves, others, life, or the world, thereby missing out on what they could possibly enjoy on a daily basis.

In a way, engaging in yoga practice alone, including the physical, emotional, mental, and spiritual sides of it, opens a door to comprehensive healing and self-care.

Joining a weekly class, doing a weekend seminar, buying a DVD – either of these will teach us postures that we can practice at our own leisure. We can pick three to five yoga exercises and do them in the morning when we get up – it does not have to be more than five to ten minutes to get started. We can make these a habit first and add relaxation and meditation once we know the postures well. Starting our day this way will determine how the rest of the day is going to turn out because our mindset will be more positive and focused.

Getting our body moving does not need to be torture but needs to fit our body, personality, and lifestyle. Nobody knows better what's good for us than ourselves, and we never work out to please anyone else but ourselves. We can set easy goals and go one step at a time. Whatever is doable is okay. If we start with a 5 minute walk, 10 squats, or half a minute plank twice a week, that's our choice. We simply need to consider it a building block to our health, because that is exactly what this is.

How to get your body moving – an overview

- ☼ Exercise improves memory, mood, and cognitive functions of the brain.
- ☼ Focus on what you can do, not on what you cannot do.
- ☼ Make exercise enjoyable.
- ☼ Get your heart rate going periodically one minute at a time.
- ☼ Exercise is easier with company.
- ☼ Involve your kids, it adds fun and consistency.
- ☼ Join a class.
- ☼ Yoga combines the physical, emotional, mental, and spiritual levels perfectly.
- ☼ Set easy goals, one step at a time.
- ☼ Exercising is for you, not for anyone else.

How to support your kids

The best we can do for our children is teach them the value of their body, to feed it healthy and nourishing foods, and to keep it strong and agile. Through our efforts to teach them a healthy lifestyle, we will automatically become healthier ourselves.

Introducing healthy foods when pizzas and take outs are the norm is most likely a challenge. But changes can come slowly. The more healthy dishes we introduce, the more we avoid unhealthy ones. Adding greens in meat dishes are a wonderful way to add some color to the table, especially if vegetable dishes are despised by our young ones. Beans, carrots, peas, and broccoli can be small side portions to start with, especially if kids are given a choice. And the question is not, "if" they are willing to try a vegetable, but "which one would you rather have"? Involving children in the cooking process has proven to be helpful in making them try new things. Not making them finish everything on their plate but encouraging them to at least eat five bites of their veggies may be another useful strategy. It's important to avoid struggles and pressure. The more consistently vegetables are on their plates, the more consistently they are exposed to them, and the more likely they will eventually not just give them a try but also eat them without hesitation or even ask for them.

Buying chips, candy, and ice cream instead of dips, nuts, and fruits is harming our kids. If we don't have junk food at home, they can't eat it there. If we offer them healthy snacks instead, they will eventually get used to these as well. Discipline starts with us parents; our kids learn from us. We must remind ourselves that we are modeling behaviors to our children 24/7. They see how we snack, eat, and exercise, and this is naturally going to be their normal as well, because that is what they know.

Being active with our children brings us much closer and shows them other ways of spending time apart from video games and social media. While they may fight inside or outside activities away from their electronics at first, they usually end up enjoying them, begging for more. Even if it doesn't seem like it, our children need our company and want to spend time with us but very often have got used to parents not having any spare time for them and possibly also spending their time passively watching TV shows or simply being on their phones. Dedicating a certain amount of time to our children to engage in joint activities will increase communication, trust, and simply fun times that everybody in the family needs.

Activities can be the ones mentioned in the previous chapter or going to amusement parks, which also involves a lot of walking and has an additional fun component. Whatever we do, we need to enjoy our children and teach them how important health is, and that self-care can also be a lot of fun. Otherwise they will pay the price for our negligence later in life.

How to support your kids – an overview

- Teach children the value of their body and health.
- Introduce healthy foods to take place of unhealthy foods – one at a time.
- Don't buy what you don't want your children to eat.
- Get your kids moving by moving with them.
- Turn off the TV and put down your phone.
- Discipline starts with parents.

CHAPTER 4

The emotional body

The numbers on the prevalence of psychiatric disorders and depression vary, but whichever report you look at, they are huge nevertheless. Dr. Mark Hyman states that 60 million Americans have been diagnosed with a psychiatric disorder. 40 million Americans suffer from anxiety and 20 million from depression. According to Dr. Daniel Amen, 51% of Americans will suffer mental illness at some point. He also looks at mental issues from a holistic perspective and has established a link between obesity, heart disease, diabetes, depression, and sleep apnea.

Sugar has been highly related to mood swings, since it affects the neurotransmitter dopamine in the brain; it is very addictive, acts as an opioid, and prevents healing. 80-90% of processed food contains added sugar. According to Hyman, children nowadays consume 34 teaspoons of sugar a day, when the recommended daily amount of refined sugar is only six teaspoons. It is very easy to exceed the recommended amount, considering that one cup of fruit yogurt, which is generally considered a health food, contains more sugar than a can of coke or two donuts. When children drink one can of soda a day their risk of obesity increases by 60%. High fructose corn syrup especially may lead to obesity, diabetes, inflammation, and nutritional deficiencies. It has also been linked to lower IQ, anxiety, aggression, hyperactivity, depression, fatigue, learning difficulties, PMS, and dementia. It reacts with proteins and creates plaques in the brain that damage brain cells and tissue[1].

A diet based on processed and junk food lacks nutrients and leads to chronic malnutrition, resulting in malnourished brains that will not function effectively, naturally impacting our thoughts and feelings alike. Some organizations report that there is also a link between GMOs and depression and anxiety, and as stated above, GMOs are found in 70-80% of processed foods. Bernie Siegel states that 90% of disease stem from thoughts and feelings. To sum things up, poor nutrition harms the body as well as the brain, and the affected brain harms the body even more.

Sources of stress

Another factor impacting our emotional state is stress. When experiencing any type of stress, the hormones cortisol and adrenaline are released in the body to prepare for possible danger. It affects heart rate, blood pressure, blood sugar levels, blood fats, and respiration, and can lead to heart disease, anxiety, depression, hypertension, and gastrointestinal disorders. Once the perceived danger has passed, these levels are supposed to go down to normal levels again. However, in modern society stress becomes continuous due to a lack of balance and physical and mental rest in daily life. Constantly elevated stress levels affect our immune system, mood, feelings of well-being and happiness, language development, and memory. Lifestyle changes are necessary, otherwise stress will lead to illness, physical burnout, inability to perform effectively at home and at work, dissatisfaction in life, and complete exhaustion. Hyman even states that cortisol shrinks the brain and kills brain cells, leading to depression and dementia. However, watching TV, having a drink, and going shopping do not suffice to relax our system properly. It takes active relaxation like meditation, yoga, deep breathing, making love, exercise, or simply sleep to bring about a beneficial relaxation response (59).

Stress is a very wide term that can mean so many different things. Simple stressors can be situational: a lot to do at work, an exam at school or in college, or a decision to be made at home. Ongoing stressors are usually very complex and mostly pertain to relationships. Relationships affect every part of our life: family, friends, coworkers, bosses, and associates. We have expectations and get our feelings hurt. We make assumptions and get our feelings hurt. We feel neglected and ignored and get our feelings hurt. We feel disrespected and get our feelings hurt. We feel treated unfairly and get our feelings hurt. Bottom line is: we get our feelings hurt way too often. Relationships have an enormous impact on us, to the point that if a close friend is overweight we are more likely to become overweight as well. Similarly, if we have a good friend with a healthy lifestyle, we are more likely to adopt that lifestyle as well. But how do we get our feelings hurt all the time and experience so much stress because of it?

If we focus on other people too much and judge WHAT they do and HOW they do what they do, we expect them to do things the way WE do them rather than letting them venture out freely on their own. In this statement alone, we have words like "judge" and "expect" and find underlying assumptions and lack of acceptance. We are acting from a place of righteousness and control rather than love and positive regard. In fact, it does not even need to matter to us what our family and friends do and how they do it, unless they are causing us or themselves any harm. Wanting to control others and not being able to, causes a lot of stress and falsely gives us the impression that our feelings get hurt when all it really is, is an offended ego. If we learned to love instead of judging, ask instead of expecting, clarify instead of assuming, and simply accept others where they are on their own personal journey, we would feel so much more at peace and reduce our sense of stress, and hurt feelings, greatly. To make progress we need to start loving and accepting ourselves on our own journey and work on our spirituality and faith to become more loving and accepting towards others as well. Letting go of control is key and not only frees up a lot of time and energy that we can then spend on self-improvement, but also makes room for more happiness in our lives.

When we reach the point of allowing others to be themselves, we need to free ourselves from people who do not offer us the same grace. We need to surround ourselves with healthy, supportive, loving, and understanding people who, just by being around us, further our own development and growth. If we are surrounded by negative, hurtful, judging, and controlling people, we get stunted, sad, stuck, and angry because we feed off them, and our stress level increases drastically. It may hurt having to let go of some people we thought we were close to, however, what really hurts is figuring out that we were not as close to them, and they were not as close to us as we thought. If we are expected to change our personality and behavior to please others so they like us, there is something wrong, and that relationship is very lopsided. Being able to be ourselves and not having to hold back or change our behavior around the people we are close to, is freeing and destressing, and these are relationships we will benefit from going forward.

Another source of stress is work. We may feel stressed due to relationships at work with bosses, managers, and coworkers or due to a workload that feels unmanageable. If stress is due to others at the job, the situation may improve when we begin working on self-value, boundaries, and communication skills. But the same principles apply as with any other relationship: we need to let go of judgment, expectations, and assumptions and accept others for where they are in life, but we do not have to like them. Not liking them does not give us the right to disrespect or fight them, though. Even if others at work are obnoxious, spiteful, or demeaning, we need to focus on simply doing our job to the best of our abilities and not taking any stabs from outside personally, no matter how personal they feel. Same with our workload, we always must do the best we can, and we can only hope that someone will notice our ambition and dedication. However, if we consistently do the best we can but still do not get the appreciation and respect we deserve, we may need to consider changing our job. A constantly negative work environment, where we spend so many more hours than anywhere else every day, is bound to affect us physically, emotionally, mentally, and spiritually. No job is important enough to get sick over. Ultimately, we grow through the experience, we learn what we do not want in our daily life, and hopefully we can find a more positive work environment going forward, knowing what to look out for and what to avoid.

A big stressor in many people's lives are finances. With constantly rising costs of living it gets harder and harder to make ends meet. Too many people live from paycheck to paycheck and do not know how to cut down expenses. Education is costly, and furthering your education comes with increased debt that needs to be repaid. When costs for housing, utilities, healthcare, car, and phone, all of which are necessities in our society, cannot be minimized any further, and ends still do not meet, the perceived stress will go through the roof. Many people can still cut down on costs for TV service, eating out, Starbucks, and little treats that are supposed to ease our perceived stress but in reality, make matters worse, due to additional money spent. Others may try to give their children things they cannot afford because they feel guilty for not being able to provide luxuries that other kids may have. However, children can be happy and appreciative without those goodies we gladly hand out to ease our guilt, and we are the ones who must teach them. We need to be very honest with ourselves. Sometimes we can save money because we spend more than we think. We can learn to appreciate what we have rather than focusing on what we want. When we appreciate what we have, we will stop yearning for more and contently work with what we have. The more we want, the more our energy aligns with the concept of wanting rather than having, and our feeling of lacking will be stronger. Our financial situation will not change if we stress over it, so we can just as well accept it and make the best of what we have. There are people who are entirely content with what little they have and manage to treasure every day nevertheless. They still move forward and are determined to live a worthwhile life. If we are calmer, happier, and feel good about our lives, solutions are much easier come by, and we stay healthy at the same time. That said, accepting where we are at this very moment in our lives does not mean that we must not strive towards abundance. It simply keeps us healthier and happier in the present moment while we pursue our goals.

When clients come to my office with excessive anxiety about anything they can possibly imagine, the first thing I ask them is whether they watch the news every day. Media has an enormous impact on our minds and emotions. All we see day in and day out is murder, conflict, political struggles, financial problems, apartment buildings burnt down, war, women being raped, catastrophes, and shocking stories. Naturally, these stories play on and on in our minds and affect our sense of safety. Media also teaches us how to talk bad about others, and society reflects that brilliantly. People talk bad about other people because it makes them feel better about themselves and distracts from their own shortcomings. Politics nowadays seems just like that. Rather than focusing on what good the politicians want to do, most of them stress how bad and incompetent the opposing party is. Basically, it seems that many of us vote for the candidate that is louder and pictured in a less negative light than the other because they are better at diverting the negative attention onto their opponent, rather than making sure to pick the candidate whose programs seem more beneficial for us. If we continuously expose ourselves to the negativity of the news, it will carry over into our emotional body and present itself as anxiety and depression due to the stress it causes and fundamental fear it triggers.

Finally, aging is a stressor that is very common when bodies start behaving differently than they used to, our looks begin to change and we notice it every time we see our reflection in the mirror, or we reach retirement age and don't know what to do with ourselves and our time. It is important to find things to do that make sense to us and give us meaning and purpose, besides our career, ahead of time. While we are still part of the workforce we need to be careful to not make our job our sole identity, otherwise we will end up lost and stripped of the reason why we get up every morning once we retire. We have to love ourselves every step of the way, accepting changes as they come, seeing them as signs of growth, and being grateful for the experiences we were blessed to make in our lifetime – even the challenging ones we learned from and managed to overcome; after all, they made us who we are today.

The emotional body – *an overview*

- Sugar has been linked to mood swings.
- Processed and junk foods lack nutrients and affect our brains negatively.
- GMOs appear to be linked to depression and anxiety.
- Stress leads to anxiety and depression.
- Relationships have a huge impact on our emotional state.
- Judgment, expectations, assumptions, and need for control increase stress.
- Acceptance of oneself and others decreases stress.
- Stress at work can be due to relationships or work load.
- Be honest about your financial needs.
- Practice appreciation and gratitude for what you have even if it is not a lot.
- Negativity in the media leads to anxiety and stress.

How to feel what you want to feel

Our family environment naturally has a profound impact on our perception of well-being. A home needs to be peaceful, welcoming, joyful, and supportive. We need to create good moments with our loved ones and have time for each other. Non-judgmental conversations are necessary on a regular basis, with our full attention on the other person to show them that they are important to us. Let's turn off the TV, put our phones down, and be together every day at least for a little while. Love is a give and take, and that is also true for families. Everybody is part of this organization and needs to chime in. We live together, sleep together, eat together, and breathe together, and it is important that everyone gets the chance to contribute and that everyone is open for compromise based on love and acceptance. Our differences do not need to cause arguments or battles for control, instead they can enhance our lives. Parents teach their children tolerance and unconditional positive regard through their own open mindset, and if they do not, children will attempt to assume control and prove their parents wrong, no matter what. Daily fights and tension will lead to personal stress and will have physical and emotional consequences. If we feel that our children are too selfish and are not behaving like an integral part of our family, we need to look at ourselves first and assess if they have learned from us what they are living now before we look for outside influences that might have brought on these changes in their behavior.

Proper organization of our living space is crucial. Our home reflects who we are. If there is chaos in our homes, that is usually how it looks inside of us as well. If it seems neat and tidy, but drawers and cabinets are in disorder, we play our role fairly well, appearing to others as if we were in a good place, when inside we may be breaking. Cleaning out our living space brings about a sense of relief, we can breathe again and feel like our world is getting bigger. Throwing out the clutter is like letting go of unnecessary baggage, hurt, and pain, finally moving forward in life again. There is happiness in a clean and organized home environment.

Part of organizing our home is creating schedules and routines in our daily life, which also creates a sense of order and control. A morning meditation, yoga session, exercising, or walking to start off the day would be a perfect example for establishing a routine in our lives. These activities can vary but need to be scheduled at about the same time every morning to jumpstart the day, get body and mind moving, and set the tone for the rest of the day. It does not take all that much, except consistency and, for some, getting up 15 minutes earlier, which doesn't sound hard but can be a huge challenge. Therefore, finding an incentive for this morning routine, such as having a peaceful place with candles and music for our exercises or a morning smoothie – or coffee – after our walk, may do the trick. We must experiment with what motivates us to do what we know is not just good for us but essential.

More satisfaction at work is linked to increased psychological health. It is important to consider ways of finding more satisfaction at work without trying to change anybody else. We need to accept bosses and coworkers the way they are; again, we don't have to like them. But what we can do is organize our workspace, putting little reminders on our desks that inspire us and remind us why we are doing what we are doing, so we can appreciate our job more. Organization at work will reflect on how we feel when we are there. It will give us a sense of control and calmness. A job is only a means to an end. We need a job to live our lives fully, not the other way around. If our work environment remains unbearable, we may need to consider a job or even career change.

An after-work routine can also be put in place for additional self-care, such as going to the gym, going for a swim, sitting in our backyard, having tea or coffee with our friends, or whatever else our heart desires. We do have a few minutes to spare, and we deserve to enjoy these few minutes. Setting priorities is highly important, and self-care is usually at the bottom of the list. Being aware of the benefits of self-care and learning to love ourselves enough is key to establish a healthy routine. Using a calendar and adding these 15 minutes – or even 30 minutes – may help to follow through consistently.

Studies have shown that satisfying hobbies lead to increased psychological health and improved coping skills at work. However, many people believe that they don't have time for hobbies, claim they have no interest, or just don't know what they want to do because they are exhausted and lack self-care. Some will benefit from remembering what they would have loved to do 10 or 20 years ago but never got around to doing it. They could start right there and see if this is still something they would like to do today. If they do, great! If they don't, just as well. We need to start exploring our likes and dislikes somewhere. If we have neglected ourselves for an extended period, we are out of touch with who we are and what makes us happy and need to go on a search. We need to find out what is fun for us and start enjoying life a little more.

Prioritizing is also important in the sense of doing only one thing at a time rather than thinking about what is the next thing to do, while still working on the first. This goes hand in hand with mindfulness, which is being discussed in the following section: we need to be present in the moment and focused on what we are doing while we are doing it. Similarly, prioritizing is the decision to stay in the here and now and dedicate our precious time and focus to one specific task that we chose to do. We will ultimately work faster and more precisely that way, and our task will not stress us as would be the case if we were doing one thing while already thinking of the next.

If our time is really so short that we cannot get everything done ourselves, what stops us from asking for help? It is okay to delegate chores and admit that we cannot do everything alone. No one needs to be a superhero, and certainly no one is. There is no pride, we simply need to be honest with ourselves and acknowledge our limits. This will not make us a lesser person, rather to the contrary. We need a good support system that can consist of family, friends, neighbors, church, or non-profit organizations that help people in need. Knowing we can rely on others to be with us during tough times is a safety blanket that allows us to stay on target in our life. Even if we feel entirely alone at times, usually there is that one person who cares for us if we allow them to.

Having multiple roles, such as spouse, parent, child, friend, worker, volunteer, and caretaker, has been correlated to increased happiness and contentment in life. However, balance must be maintained, allowing for self-expression through talents, interests, work, and relationships. Self-care and leisure, as well as a satisfying work experience, are crucial components of satisfaction in addition to our various roles and must not be overlooked. An overload of roles and tasks in life, however, leads to stress, exhaustion, depression, and can affect our physical health, while balanced roles increase self-esteem, feelings of accomplishment, and happiness[2]. Having balanced roles, taking care of ourselves, and cultivating serious hobbies will benefit us as we get older because we can find satisfaction in different areas of our life as we do, and when we retire we have plenty of roles and hobbies to fall back on.

Forms of relaxation

Meditation has been widely suggested as a great relaxation technique, however, many people have no clue how to go about it. They may not know where to start, their brains don't turn off, or they are reluctant to try it out because it appears to go against their religion. Clearing our mind of everything around us is very difficult to achieve with all the impressions we receive on a daily basis. One way to meditation is through mindfulness. Mindfulness is not emptying our mind, it is rather the opposite: a sharpened focus on what is surrounding us. We use our senses, seeing, hearing, smelling, tasting, and feeling, to take it all in, this again distracts us completely from our random thought processes. Mindfulness brings us into the present moment and helps us live our lives in the here and now, the only place there is. The past is long gone, and the future may never come.

Mindfulness can be practiced in the room where we are sitting, outside in nature, and even while washing our dishes. The importance lies in being aware of what we are doing and what that feels like. Washing our dishes while seeing the water, hearing the water, smelling the soap, tasting the food we have eaten, and feeling the process of wiping the dishes and the water running over our hands will help us wash our dishes faster because we stop our negative thoughts about how much we dislike what we are doing. The point is to keep pushing away any thoughts whenever they pop into our heads and refocusing on our surrounding and what we are doing in this very moment, being completely present in the here and now. Mindfulness results in a positive feeling and calmness.

Another way to practice mindfulness is to visualize a happy place by picturing a place from memory or one we would like to see and immersing ourselves with all our senses. This can be a wonderful modification when age causes our senses to weaken. Creating and holding on to good memories, as well as surrounding ourselves with images of beautiful places that inspire us, like hanging pictures on the walls of our home or books about the places we love, will enable us to practice this relaxation technique at any age.

Mindfulness has shown to decrease not only anxiety but also depression, stress-related physical symptoms, and feelings of physical pain, thereby improving life quality, relationships, general feeling of health and well-being, sleep, immune function, emotional life, and the ability to have positive feelings and deal with difficult situations. It is also helpful for substance abuse disorders. There are mobile apps available that can assist with meditation and mindfulness techniques. Mindfulness works on all four levels of the body, leading to improved wellness in physical, emotional, mental, and spiritual, as well as relationship matters. Studies have shown mindfulness to impact brain health by balancing neurotransmitter activity, thereby reducing anxiety and agitation, when practiced as little as twelve minutes a day. This indicates that there is brain plasticity, meaning that brains can change and adjust based on input of not only diet but also experiences.

On a side note, the notion of brain plasticity is highly important when trauma and abuse lead to impacted self-awareness, self-evaluation, and emotional regulation[3] due to changes in the brain in regard to stress responses, elevated levels of pro-inflammatory cytokines, and their effect on the neurotransmitters serotonin, dopamine, and glutamate[4]. There is hope for trauma victims to heal if they take care of themselves on every level of their being. Structural changes in the brain resulting from therapy are indeed measurable and can occur even in old age, including building new neurons and new connections in the learning process. In addition to diet that nourishes our brain, mindfulness and meditation to find balance, and learning to focus on our thoughts and feelings, we need therapy to work on processing past experiences and find words to express what is going on in our minds. Exercise is also crucial to keep our brains expanding by increasing blood flow and the release of serotonin. The changes in our minds achieved this way allow behavior changes to follow[5]. Since brain plasticity can be observed at any age, our efforts to take care of our brain need to be ongoing even at an older age, when many people seem to believe that there is no use to continue any work to enhance and maintain our memory and cognitive functions.

Breathing techniques, even without prior experience with meditation, yoga, and mindfulness-based cognitive therapy, have shown to help with depressed mood when antidepressants were ineffective. They reduce stress and change brain waves[6]. It is beneficial to slow down our breathing and briefly hold our breath. There are various techniques that specify for how long we have to hold our breath. One simple version is to breathe in to the count of four, hold our breath to the count of four, breathe out to the count of four, and hold our breath again to the count of four. Doing this for three to four minutes will have a calming effect and reduces stress.

Coping skills for emotional well-being

The importance of exercise and yoga has been discussed in the previous chapter. They benefit our physical and emotional bodies the same. Moving our body changes brain chemistry and gives us a happy and elated feeling, which again increases the likelihood to maintain a consistent practice. This clearly shows the holistic nature of physical activity, which benefits all four bodies simultaneously.

Coping skills for emotional well-being can be anything that involves the five senses: seeing, hearing, smelling, tasting, and feeling. When using these coping skills, it's also important to maintain our focus on what we are doing and consistently keep pushing away any thoughts that may come up without any frustration. It's okay for thoughts to come into our minds; it is not okay to let them linger or take over. The following are simple ideas to change the way we feel in the moment:

- *Seeing:* coloring, painting, sitting on the patio and watching nature, watching a funny show, doing a puzzle, reading funny stories, looking at photographs to remind ourselves of happy memories.
- *Hearing:* listen to music, an audio book, sounds of nature, a meditation CD; playing an instrument.
- *Smelling:* using scented candles, bath salts and essential oils; eating food; cooking, baking.
- *Tasting:* eating, drinking, brushing teeth, using mouthwash.
- *Feeling:* working out and sweating, taking a shower or bath, getting a massage, manicure or pedicure, simply resting, being mindfully aware of our surroundings.

In therapy, I use a technique called REMAP, developed by Steve Reed, a psychotherapist, who uses acupressure points to help get rid of emotions attached to negative memories. These acupressure points stimulate the limbic system in the brain, which is where the emotions sit that tend to take over and prevent the thinking brain from functioning when traumatic memories are triggered. I have seen clients change their perspective of a highly traumatic event in their lives within only a few sessions, being able to detach from the feelings they experienced when the trauma occurred. Once they learn how to use this technique by themselves, they can apply it independently at home whenever they need to.

Basically, anything that feels good is allowed, as long as we don't hurt ourselves or anyone else. It is important to be able to take care of our needs on our own in case we hit a low and nobody happens to be around to help. Of course, when things are rough it is okay – and beneficial – to involve friends and family if they are available. However, being able to control our emotions and change them when they pull us down will support a positive sense of self and a feeling of strength because we do not need to rely on others to make us feel better. Increased self-esteem and self-love result from allowing us to take care of ourselves, controlling our thoughts, which will be discussed in a later chapter, and being on a spiritual path. The more we are there for ourselves, the better we will feel about our lives. The better we feel about our lives, the more optimistic we will be. We can learn to gain trust in ourselves and determine who else we can trust in life. The more independent we are, the less we need to rely on others, the less we expect from them, the less we get disappointed, and the more we can trust people close to us who have earned it over time.

How to feel what you want to feel – *an overview*

- Home environment is a crucial factor in wellbeing.
- It is okay to ask for help when you need help.
- Allow people to be part of your support system.
- Multiple roles in life can add to positive feelings, however, too many can be overwhelming.
- Keep your personal space clean and organized.
- Schedules and routines benefit your emotional wellbeing.
- Improve your work environment.
- Find a hobby that gives you joy.
- Do one thing at a time.
- One way to meditation can be through mindfulness.
- Mindfulness decreases anxiety, depression, stress, and pain.
- Slow down your breathing to calm down.
- Exercise and yoga benefit your physical and emotional bodies.
- Use coping skills that involve your five senses.
- Learn to control your emotions and change them in the moment.
- Emotional independence leads to self-love and trust.
- The brain can heal and improve after trauma and injury through diet, relaxation, thought processes, and self-care.

How to support your kids

First and foremost, kids need to eat healthy and nutrient-dense foods. If we feed them junk foods, their mood will be negatively impacted. Reducing their intake of fast food on one hand and sugar on the other, and replacing these with healthier food choices will morph our kids into happier, more balanced, more nourished, and healthier children – once their fight for their junk foods is wearing down. Habit is such a big factor in diet choices, and so are peers, parents' time constraints, and daily stress. Preparing healthy food does not have to be hard or take a lot of time. If we do our grocery shopping on weekends and cut up part of the meat and vegetables for the following week, the cooking process itself can be very brief. It only involves some planning and determination to follow through. Even if we change our habits for three or four days of the week and stick to old habits the other days, there is improvement and added nutrition. Chances are that getting used to eating some healthier foods may create cravings for nutrient-dense foods not only because the body wants more of it but also because we think about our health and options more. We model behavior for our children, so if we change our own eating habits and let them be part of it by explaining why we do what we do, they may get interested in doing the same. Kids need to understand the challenges we face in finding the right path through the food mess in our society. In addition, making time for family meals, sitting at the table, and eating together will not only improve our eating habits but also family dynamics and communication.

Having regular family talks is important for the emotional well-being of all family members. We get closer, and we develop more understanding for and acceptance of each other when we express interest in what our children say and do. We need to make sure to turn off any outside distractions such as TVs and phones and show our interest for and dedication to our kids. They will learn from us that doing so will show respect to others. We need to routinely invite our children to communicate with us, even if they are hiding out in their rooms or stuck on their electronics. We can always pop our head in there to merely check in with them. There will be times when they have shut down and other times when they suddenly open up. If we as parents don't consistently put effort into checking in with our children, the chances of them emerging from their cave are much smaller.

A wonderful way to keep family communication going is the weekly family meeting. Of course, this can be scheduled twice a week or even every other day if the need arises. All family members take part in these meetings, and everybody is encouraged to express one or more good things about the others, and one thing they would like them to work on, talking to each person one at a time and for the rest of the family to hear. The tone of each speaker needs to be friendly or matter-of-fact, non-critical, and non-judgmental. The other person needs to avoid being defensive and justifying their actions. There is no right or wrong. All that matters is how the person who brings up a specific situation feels about it, and their feelings need to be acknowledged. Then they feel heard, and the discussion can lead to problem solving and finding ways on how to deal with specific situations differently. Everybody can express themselves without fear of being criticized or hurting the other one's feelings. In this manner, the first person addresses every other family member one at a time. Once their turn is over, the next person does the same and so on. From what I have seen in these meetings, parents learn to listen, acknowledge, and validate their children's perspectives and feelings, which in turn makes kids more comfortable speaking up about their personal concerns because they do not need to be afraid of being punished for having an opinion that differs from their parents' point of view. They learn to address issues with their parents constructively, and parents learn to not fall into the "I'm the parent, you're the child – so be quiet and listen" trap.

Many children deal with a lot of stress related to school, homework, friends, and parents. We need to teach them how to deal with stress and how to balance it. This can be in form of time management skills, helping them to develop a daily routine, problem-solving, mindfulness and meditation techniques, breathing techniques, or simply talking to them regularly. When children feel anxiety or stress they are usually open for suggestions to reduce their uncomfortable feelings. Involving them in physical activities like riding bikes together, sharing a hobby, taking them out to have ice-cream, going to the movies, cleaning out the garage, washing a car, all help to balance their stress with active involvement and invite for further communication. Allowing their friends to come over so we can meet them gives us an opportunity to get to know them better and to find out what our kids' social environment looks like. Parents often expect respect from their children without showing them respect on their part. I tend to tell parents if they show their children respect they will learn to do the same. After all, parents always model behavior, and children always learn. Stress with parents, which can be anything from chores to friends to lack of respect, can all be addressed in above-mentioned family meetings. These meetings can teach our children fundamental communication skills, which they will be able to apply in their current and future personal and professional relationships; they are practically life lessons.

Respect also shows itself in how parents enforce consequences when their kids mess up. If their consequence is grounding them and not allowing them to use the car, parents cannot punish their teen for not picking up their siblings from school or sports practice and leaving them stranded. If their consequence is to ground their teen from their laptop, they cannot punish them for not being able to complete their homework and getting an email from their teacher about missing work. Consequences must be logical and proactive, kids need to learn from them and understand them, and there needs to be a calm and collected conversation about the situation without any yelling and expression of anger. This is one form to show respect – not to put our children into a lose-lose situation. We clearly lose that way too, increasing everybody's stress level. Kids will get scared of us or, even worse, develop resentment towards us, leading to more mess-ups and worse choices due to their feeling of not being able to get it right anyway.

We need to appreciate our children, tell them how much we love them, tell them how happy they make us, and catch them being good! They deserve to be seen and validated. They need to be. We need to hold on to positive memories when they were small, talk about memories created together, look at old photographs and videos, create new memories, tell them about our past, and share our music with them, while listening to theirs also. All that makes the family structure stronger and creates a happier home environment. We need to be aware of what they watch on TV or the Internet, explain what they have seen if we find out that they watched something we rather wish they hadn't. We can watch shows and movies together, including documentaries about touchy subjects so we can put this information in context and see how it applies in their lives and environment. Our kids know about sex, they know about LGBT social movements for our lesbian-gay-bisexual-transgender population, they know about drugs, and they know kids who are involved in either one or all of them. Open, non-judgmental conversation about current issues such as sexuality and drugs is hugely important and may keep them on a healthy path.

How to support your kids – an overview

- Feed your kids healthy foods, avoid junk food.
- Reduce the sugar your kids consume.
- Start implementing changes gradually.
- Remember that we model eating behaviors as well.
- Sit down and eat with your kids.
- Talk to your kids regularly and with your full attention on them.
- Implement family meetings to give your kids a voice.
- Teach your kids stress management.
- Get active with them.
- Respect goes both ways.
- Make consequences for their behavior logical and workable.
- Share positive memories and create new ones.
- Appreciate and enjoy your children.

CHAPTER 5

The mental body

This chapter contains an overview of how nutrition and physical ailments can affect our brain function and consequently our mental health. This overview is followed by practical coping skills that focus on learning how to control our daily thought processes. It is crucial to keep these body-brain connections in mind when making food choices, because we need good brain health to be able to fully apply the coping skills discussed that have the potential to change our lives for good.

Not too long ago I had an experience that illustrates this body-brain connection perfectly. Having lived on breads, pasta, and pizza nearly all my life, I decided to finally improve my diet. I experimented with smoothies, used ingredients like greens, nuts, seeds, avocados, blueberries, non-dairy milk, and apple cider vinegar. For a short period of time I would have two large smoothies a day, which were quite filling, so I did not eat much in addition to these. After one week, my body was going through detox, I felt uncomfortable, my belly was shaped in a way I had never seen it before, but I waited it out. The discomfort only lasted for a couple days, and I continued drinking my smoothies. After two weeks, I felt a drastic change in my mind: my mood was upbeat, I had much more energy, I could think much more clearly, and I was motivated and happy. Suddenly I could go through a day without feeling fatigued, I got so much more done, and I simply felt happy to be alive. I continued living healthy, and while I did not notice much change over the next few months, the extent of improvement became clear later that year when I went for my yearly visit to see my family in Europe. The happiness and joy I felt being there that time was much more intense than any year before. My energy level was through the roof the entire time I was there, and my mood was much more stable. I barely recognized myself. Consequently, I have continued on this path ever since, which is not hard to do since my body craves nutritious foods more than ever. I make myself remember the times when I felt low, depressed, fatigued, and unmotivated to keep myself from making unhealthy choices I would only regret later. That said, I do allow myself treats now and then, but honestly, my cravings for sweets and salty snacks are currently not what they used to be and rarely show up at all.

Vitamins and minerals

Lack of nutrients affects mental health. This section lists the main vitamins and minerals and how deficiencies can affect us mentally. This is not a complete list and is meant to make the reader aware of the importance of eating healthy and which foods to pick to provide the body the best nutrition possible. A shortened overview of vitamins, minerals, and foods in which they can be found is added at the end of this section.

Vitamin A deficiency leads to fatigue, irritability, loss of appetite, and headaches. Vitamin A rich foods are beef liver, carrots, sweet potato, kale, spinach, apricots, broccoli, butter, eggs, and winter squash.

Vitamin B deficiencies, especially niacin (or vitamin B3), vitamin B6, folate (or vitamin B9), and vitamin B12, may lead to cognitive dysfunction and mood swings. Folate is linked to various mental disorders and nervous system defects, such as autism, schizophrenia, attention problems, and language delays. Studies suggest that deficiencies in utero impair the fetus's brain development and gene regulation. Studies, however, do not show clearly whether it is the vitamin deficiency that leads to autism or antibodies that block folate from being absorbed. When affected children received a chemical form of folate that was not attacked by antibodies, their autism symptoms diminished. Being precursors of serotonin and dopamine, two important neurotransmitters involved in mood regulation, folate and vitamins B6 and B12 appear to help with depression and bipolar disorder. Another result of folate deficiency seems to be obesity. Folate can be found in dark leafy greens, especially spinach, Garbanzo and Pinto beans, lentils, black eyed peas, broccoli, liver, asparagus, avocado, beets, oranges, papayas, bananas, and cantaloupe[1]. Vitamin B6 rich foods are turkey breast, grass-fed beef, pistachios, tuna, Pinto beans, avocado, blackstrap molasses, sunflower seeds, and sesame seeds. Vitamin B12 rich foods are beef liver, sardines, Atlantic mackerel, lamb, nutritional yeast, feta cheese, grass-fed beef, cottage cheese, and eggs. Niacin has shown improvement in dementia and behavior in individuals with Niacin deficiency[2]. Niacin rich foods are turkey, chicken breast, peanuts, mushrooms, liver, tuna, green peas, grass-fed beef, sunflower seeds, and avocado.

Vitamin D is best absorbed when being exposed to the sun, however, the use of sunscreen blocks the vitamin D production in the skin. Vitamin D is essential for most systems in the body, helps with preserving memory, clears out toxins implicated in Alzheimer's disease, and reduces cognitive decline and dementia. Prenatal vitamin D is crucial for nerve cells and brain development in the fetus. Schizophrenia appears to be negatively impacted by a deficiency in vitamin D. Very few foods contain this vitamin, such as salmon and sardines[3].

Vitamin E deficiency can lead to dizziness and sensory changes. Vitamin E rich foods are almonds, spinach, sweet potato, avocado, wheat germ, sunflower seeds, palm oil, butternut squash, trout, and olive oil.

Iron deficiency has been linked to fatigue and impaired mental functioning. Iron rich foods are spirulina (a blue-green algae), liver, grass-fed beef, lentils, dark chocolate, spinach, sardines, pistachios, and raisins.

Manganese and copper deficiencies have been linked to abnormal brain function. Foods rich in manganese are leafy green vegetables, blueberries, blackberries, pineapple, strawberries, loganberries, raspberries, whole grains, legumes, nuts, spices like cloves, cardamom, ginger, salt, basil and pumpkin pie spice, fish and shellfish, tea and coffee, molasses, cocoa, maple syrup, and pumpkin seeds. Copper can be found in beef liver, sunflower seeds, lentils, almonds, dried apricots, dark chocolate, blackstrap molasses, asparagus, mushrooms, and turnip greens.

Zinc deficiency can lead to apathy, irritability, fatigue, and neurological impairment. Foods rich in zinc are lamb, pumpkin seeds, grass-fed beef, chickpeas, cocoa powder, cashew nuts, kefir and yogurt, mushrooms, spinach, and chicken.

Magnesium is important to protect the brain and possibly prevent Alzheimer's disease and memory loss. It may even be able to reverse cognitive deficits of Alzheimer's. A deficiency of magnesium may lead to depression, anxiety, restlessness, nervousness, apathy, insomnia, muscle spasms, headaches, increased levels of inflammation, strokes, high blood sugar, diabetes, and insulin resistance. Many foods lose magnesium when being processed. In addition to that, soils are depleted, and food contains less of this mineral. Whole grains, nuts, leafy greens, vegetables, spinach, soybeans, sesame seeds, halibut, and black beans are sources of magnesium[4].

Antioxidants are said to be highly important for brain health and protect against cognitive decline, anxiety,

ADHD, autism, bipolar disorder, depression, and schizophrenia. Sources of antioxidants are vitamins A, C, and E, as well as polyphenols in foods. They are important to counteract oxidative stress, which is one of the major causes of Alzheimer's disease[5]. Polyphenols are found in plant based foods like berries, black currants, plums, cherries, apples, artichokes, chicory, red onions, spinach, cloves, cilantro, gingko biloba, turmeric, dark chocolate, beans, nuts, soy, black and green tea, coffee, and red wine.

Vitamins and minerals – *an overview*

- **Vitamin A** deficiency: fatigue, irritability, loss of appetite, headaches. Vitamin A rich foods: beef liver, carrots, sweet potato, kale, spinach, apricots, broccoli, butter, eggs, winter squash.
- **Vitamin B** deficiency: cognitive dysfunction, mood swings. Vitamin B6 rich foods: turkey breast, grass-fed beef, pistachios, tuna, Pinto beans, avocado, blackstrap molasses, sunflower seeds, sesame seeds. Vitamin B12 rich foods: beef liver, sardines, Atlantic mackerel, lamb, nutritional yeast, feta cheese, grass-fed beef, cottage cheese, eggs.
- **Folate** deficiency: autism, schizophrenia, attention problems, language delays, obesity. Folate rich foods: dark leafy greens, especially spinach, Garbanzo and Pinto beans, lentils, black eyed peas, broccoli, liver, asparagus, avocado, beets, oranges, papayas, bananas, cantaloupe.
- **Niacin** or **vitamin B3** deficiency: dementia and behavior problems. Niacin rich foods: turkey, chicken breast, peanuts, mushrooms, liver, tuna, green peas, grass-fed beef, sunflower seeds, avocado.
- **Vitamin D** deficiency: memory problems, Alzheimer's disease, dementia, schizophrenia. Vitamin D rich foods: salmon, sardines.
- **Vitamin E** deficiency: dizziness and sensory changes. Vitamin E rich foods: almonds, spinach, sweet potato, avocado, wheat germ, sunflower seeds, palm oil, butternut squash, trout, olive oil.
- **Iron** deficiency: fatigue, impaired mental functioning. Iron rich foods: spirulina, liver, grass-fed beef, lentils, dark chocolate, spinach, sardines, pistachios, raisins.
- **Manganese** and **copper** deficiency: abnormal brain function. Manganese rich foods: leafy green vegetables, blueberries, blackberries, pineapple, strawberries, loganberries, raspberries, whole grains, legumes, nuts, spices like cloves, cardamom, ginger, salt, basil and pumpkin pie spice, fish and shellfish, tea and coffee, molasses, cocoa and maple syrup, pumpkin seeds. Copper can be found in: beef liver, sunflower seeds, lentils, almonds, dried apricots, dark chocolate, blackstrap molasses, asparagus, mushrooms, turnip greens.
- **Zinc** deficiency: apathy, irritability, neurological impairment. Zinc rich foods: lamb, pumpkin seeds, grass-fed beef, chickpeas, cocoa powder, cashew nuts, kefir and yogurt, mushrooms, spinach, chicken.
- **Magnesium** deficiency: nervousness, restlessness, apathy, Alzheimer's disease, memory loss, depression, anxiety, insomnia, headaches.
- **Antioxidant** deficiency: cognitive decline, anxiety, ADHD, autism, bipolar disorder, depression, schizophrenia. Antioxidant rich foods: Vitamins A, C, and E, berries, black currants, plums, cherries, apples, artichokes, chicory, red onions, spinach, cloves, cilantro, gingko biloba, turmeric, dark chocolate, beans, nuts, soy, black and green tea, coffee, red wine.

The impact of food on neurotransmitters in our brain

In his seminar *Food for thought: How nutrients affect mental health and the brain*, Ken Goodrick pointed out astonishing links between what we eat and how our brains perform based on neurotransmitter processes. Protein, fats, vitamins, and minerals impact neurotransmitters, which among other functions regulate mood, cognition, and sleep.

Serotonin, which is linked to mood issues, major depressive disorder, OCD, sleep, migraines, ADHD, and fibromyalgia, increases with insulin production. A high-carb diet would lead to increased serotonin. However, a long-term high-carb diet would lead to insulin resistance and lower serotonin levels. A protein-rich diet is linked to low serotonin levels, which results in depression and irritation. As always, a balanced diet is key to keep our serotonin level stable. In order to produce serotonin, the body needs vitamins B6 and B12, folic acid, and tryptophan. Tryptophan, which supports a relaxed and happy mood and improves sleep, is found in chocolate, oats, dried dates, yogurt, red meat, eggs, fish, sunflower seeds, pumpkin seeds, corn, and peanuts.

Dopamine levels are linked to attention, memory, cognition, mood, sleep, and the feeling of pleasure. High levels may cause manic symptoms, while low levels may lead to social anxiety. Tyrosine, found in protein-rich foods such as chicken, fish, avocados, almonds, and yogurt, as well as in vitamin B6 and E, magnesium, iron, folate, and berries keep dopamine levels stable. Tyrosine and tryptophan cannot have high levels at the same time, when one is high the other one is low.

Selenium is an essential trace element that may alter levels of neurotransmitters in the brain. High levels of selenium in the diet appear to improve symptoms of depression and lower anxiety[6]. Selenium is found in Brazil nuts, tuna, halibut, sardines, grass-fed beef, turkey, beef liver, chicken, egg, and spinach.

Opioid peptides affect memory, motivation, mood swings, and euphoria. Sugar increases opioid activity in the brain, but it is also known to cause inflammation and believed to be more addictive than cocaine and heroin. The problem with sugar is being discussed in the next section.

Glutamate supports cognitive functions and requires protein-rich foods. Natural sources of glutamate are meats, poultry, fish, eggs, and dairy. According to Hyman, glutamate can overexcite and damage brain cells. GABA is an inhibitory neurotransmitter that is synthesized from glutamate. It is involved in relaxation and sleep; it also reduces anxiety and convulsions. Foods containing GABA are oolong tea, cherry tomatoes, shrimp, and fermented foods like kefir, kimchi, miso, sauerkraut, tempeh, and yogurt.

Acetylcholine is a neurotransmitter that helps with REM sleep and enhances sensory perceptions and attention. Choline is a fatlike substance that is converted into acetylcholine. It is found in wheat germ, eggs, chicken, organ meats, steaks, seafood, salmon, soybeans, peanuts, black beans, broccoli, and cauliflower. Reduced levels of choline lead to short-term memory loss.

The impact of food on neurotransmitters – an overview

- **Protein, fats, vitamins, and minerals** in our foods impact neurotransmitters.
- **Serotonin** impacts our mood and sleep. We need Vitamins B6 and B12, folate, and tryptophan to produce serotonin. Tryptophan is found in chocolate, oats, dried dates, yogurt, red meat, eggs, fish, sunflower seeds, pumpkin seeds, corn, and peanuts.
- **Dopamine** impacts our cognition, mood, sleep, and the feeling of pleasure. We need Vitamins B6 and E, magnesium, iron, folate, berries, and tyrosine to keep dopamine levels stable. Tyrosine is found in chicken, fish, avocados, almonds, and yogurt.
- **Selenium** helps with depression and anxiety and is found in Brazil nuts, tuna, halibut, sardines, grass-fed beef, turkey, beef liver, chicken, egg, and spinach.
- **Sugar** increases opioid activity in the brain and is more addictive than cocaine and heroin.
- **Glutamate** supports cognitive function and is found in meats, poultry, fish, eggs, and dairy.
- **GABA** is involved in relaxation and sleep. It also reduces anxiety and convulsions. GABA is synthesized from glutamate and found in oolong tea, cherry tomatoes, shrimp, and fermented foods like kefir, kimchi, miso, sauerkraut, tempeh, and yogurt.
- **Acetylcholine** helps with sleep and attention and is converted from choline. Choline is found in wheat germ, eggs, chicken, organ meats, steaks, seafood, salmon, soybeans, peanuts, black beans, broccoli, and cauliflower.

The effects of certain foods and lifestyle factors on mental health

Depression and anxiety symptoms have shown to be reduced with increased intake of fruits, vegetables, seafood, and whole grains, but worsen with increased processed foods, fried foods, sweetened drinks, and salt. Five servings of fruits and vegetables a day are recommended to reduce psychological distress and increase happiness, life satisfaction, and well-being, possibly in conjunction with lifestyle factors like physical activity[10]. Lifestyle factors contributing to depression are an unhealthy diet in general, urbanization, social inequality and isolation, loneliness, sedentary lifestyle, and sleep deprivation, all of which lead to poor physical health[11].

Getting eight to nine hours of sleep every night, as opposed to merely six to seven, will reduce the risk of depression, attention difficulties, learning difficulties, memory problems, and Alzheimer's. Sleep deficiencies also affect the hormone ghrelin, increasing the feeling of hunger. At the same time, they increase the stress hormone cortisol, which kills brain cells related to memory and mood[12].

Breakfast is associated with improved mood and memory function, while large size lunch, and dinner right before going to bed are associated with increased risk of depression. Regular meal patterns, meaning three meals a day, as well as eating slowly, drinking less fluids while eating to improve digestion, eating healthy snacks daily, and avoiding animal fats are associated with fewer mental problems and reduced depression and anxiety. It is not clear whether these behaviors improve people's mood or whether improved mood leads to healthier eating habits[13].

The association between sugar and junk food and depression has been mentioned above. Our brain needs sugar in the form of glucose. Fructose, however, is a type of sugar that our body cannot handle very well. It is primarily metabolized by the liver and increases the production of triglycerides, leading to fatty liver disease, memory deficiencies especially in males, diabetes, Alzheimer's, depression, and lack of energy[7]. Simple sugars, which are metabolized quickly and lead to a quick and brief sugar rush followed by a sudden crash, are found in fruits, milk products, and refined sugar. According to some, they also decrease cognitive function. Low sugar levels are linked to impaired judgment and cognitive function, crying, impatience, anxiety, irritability, fatigue, and aggressiveness. Self-control may be inhibited by simple sugars as well. Complex sugars like in green vegetables, whole grains, starchy vegetables, and legumes can regulate blood sugar for longer periods of time without quick surges and crashes.

Dementia and Alzheimer's have been linked to insulin resistance, metabolic syndrome, and diabetes; higher blood glucose appears to lead to reduced memory capacity[8]. Hyman points out that insulin levels rise due to high sugar intake, increase belly fat and obesity, and affect our stress hormones, thyroid hormones, and sex hormones, thus impacting our brain functions and possibly leading to depression, dementia, anxiety, and ADHD[9].

Dr. William Davis, a cardiologist, has researched the effects of gluten on the body and mind. The gliadin protein in gluten is broken down into peptides and, similar to sugar, acts as an opiate. It causes increased appetite, migraines, epilepsy, neuropathy, inflammation, arthritis, leaky gut, and a prolactin release from the pituitary gland, which leads to bigger breasts in men and women. In regard to mental health, Davis and Hyman state that gluten may be linked to

- ADD, ADHD, and decreased attention spans
- Dementia, mental fog, and difficulty concentrating
- Anger outbursts
- Food obsessions
- Hallucinations and paranoia in schizophrenics
- Mania in bipolar disorder, depression, and anxiety
- Autism

Dr. David Perlmutter, a neurologist, author, and researcher, proposes to leave gluten out of our diet entirely. He states that any type of bread, white or whole-wheat, raises our blood sugar more than table sugar, which in the long run leads to insulin resistance and a long list of physical and mental problems. He even goes further to indicate that high amounts of any carbohydrates in our diet, not just sweetened beverages and grain-based foods, but also potatoes, corn, fruit, and rice, are harmful for us and the culprit for diabetes and dementia[14].

According to Perlmutter, high-fat diets with lots of omega-3s are crucial to feed our brains properly. He also states that cholesterol is highly important for our health, serving as an antioxidant and precursor to vitamin D production, and in fact only plays a minor role in coronary heart disease[15]. Korn supports this controversial perspective, stating that cholesterol is important for hormones, omega-3s, and vitamin D, which is a fat-soluble vitamin[16].

An imbalance of the omega-6/omega-3 ratio can lead to a whole range of problems:

> ➢ Mood disturbances: depression, anxiety, and bipolar disorder
> ➢ Impaired brain function: reduced ability to cope with stress, ADD, autism, learning disabilities, and dementia
> ➢ Physical problems: inflammation, diabetes, and stroke

While the ratio should possibly be 1:1, it is nowadays more like 20:1. Omega-3s are found in seafood, fatty fish, algae, and plants. It has shown to improve behavior and learning in elementary school children, such as fewer ADHD-type behaviors and improved reading levels[17]. Low blood levels of omega-3 fatty acids have been observed in individuals with dementia. Adding omega-3 fatty acids has shown improvement in Alzheimer's disease, depression, and schizophrenia.

Polyunsaturated fats are found in salmon, vegetable oils, nuts, and seeds and have been recommended, at least in mediation, by some experts and organizations like the American Heart Association, while saturated fats, found in animal meats, have been reported to be unhealthy for mental health, cognitive function, and heart health. However, there is a lot of conflicting information on which fats are good for us and which are not. Vegetable oils used in fried foods and oils used in processed foods are associated with risk of depression and therefore not recommended by other experts and professionals[18]. The way animals were raised and fed may play a huge role in whether animal fats are beneficial for or detrimental to our health. Looking for pasture-raised and grass-fed meats will ensure that our food comes from the healthiest animals, and some experts claim that fats from these animals are good for us while fats from non-grass-fed animals are the ones that are harmful.

The fact that the fat in healthy animals differs so much from that in unhealthy ones seems to be a good indicator that inadequate diet in humans may also have negative effects on our bodies. According to various sources, healthy fats include:

- Avocados
- Nuts (walnut, almond, pistachio) and seeds (flaxseeds, chia seeds, sunflower seeds)
- Olives and olive oil
- Salmon and tuna
- Dark chocolate
- Tofu and eggs

Trans fats or hydrogenated fats, as found in processed foods, baked goods, fried foods, and margarine, on the other hand, have shown to damage cells, and lead to inflammation, ADHD, depression, and dementia[19].

Protein is needed to form neurotransmitters, but high protein diets can result in irritability and depression. The building blocks of protein are amino acids, which are found in fish, chicken, beans, nuts, and seeds. According to Hyman, every meal should contain protein in order to prevent sluggishness, fogginess, anxiety, confusion, fatigue, and depression[20].

Anxiety levels may possibly respond to:

- whole grains, oats
- beans
- bananas
- milk, cheese, soy

- poultry
- nuts, sesame, peanut butter
- reduced sugar
- reduced caffeine
- magnesium
- passionflower, and kava

ADHD is linked to low levels of dopamine, and some researchers have proposed to look for food allergies or nutrient deficiencies, such as omega-3 fatty acids, zinc, iron, and magnesium. Artificial food dyes have also been linked to ADHD, as well as trans fats, carbs, and sugar.

Oxidative stress happens when antioxidants are lacking in our diet, and it has been found to be one of the major causes of Alzheimer's disease. Cognitive impairment seems to improve with:

- ginkgo biloba, turmeric
- green tea, caffeine
- omega-3s and less saturated fat
- antioxidants
- flavonoids, which include:
  - berries, tree fruits
  - nuts
  - beans, vegetables
  - spices
  - vitamins B6, B12, D, and E
  - choline
  - copper, iron, calcium, zinc, selenium

Certain foods, such as turmeric, have wonderful qualities and can improve Alzheimer's disease, inflammation, depression, stress, insomnia, trauma, and anxiety[21]. It has also shown to protect neurons from Parkinson's disease and reduce cognitive impairment. Sage improves memory and attention, simply smelling sage can boost memory and mood. Rosemary increases the speed of working memory. The smell of peppermint and cinnamon increases alertness and reduces fatigue[22].

Food allergies have also been linked to depression, anxiety, lack of motivation, brain fog, irritability, and anger without cause[23]. Similarly, food sensitivities can lead to irritable bowel syndrome, anxiety, depression, and bipolar disorder. Getting tested not only for food allergies, but also for food sensitivities, which may not even be obvious to the affected individuals themselves, could possibly avoid future physical and mental health challenges. As mentioned before, naturopaths and functional medicine doctors use specific tests to determine whether we better avoid certain food groups in our diet. Many traditional doctors do not support this kind of testing. We need to remember that even though we may not have any reactions to certain food groups at the present moment, there can still be a sensitivity that leads to systemic inflammation in the long run, possibly resulting in chronic diseases, digestive issues, autoimmune diseases, allergies, and mental health symptoms. As mentioned before, the elimination diet and pulse test can be useful tools in identifying food sensitivities.

The effects of certain foods and lifestyle factors on mental health – an overview

- **Junk food** increases depression.
- When struggling with **depression and anxiety**, eat more fruits and vegetables. Avoid processed foods, sugar, and caffeine.
- When struggling with **depression**, eat regular meals, eat them slowly, make good lifestyle choices.
- **Sugar** increases depression and reduces cognitive function. Fructose is linked to memory deficiencies, Alzheimer's disease, depression, and fatigue.
- **Whole grains** can regulate blood sugar for longer periods of time.
  Low blood sugar leads to impaired judgment and cognitive function, depressed mood, anxiety, irritability, and fatigue.
  High blood sugar also leads to depression and cognitive impairment.
- **Diabetes** has been linked to dementia and Alzheimer's disease.
- **Gluten** act as an opiate and are linked to ADD, ADHD, anger, attention, hallucinations, depression, anxiety, dementia, and autism.
- **Omega-3** deficiency: depression, stress, impaired brain function.
  Omega-3 rich foods: seafood, fatty fish, algae, plants.
- **Good fats**: avocados, nuts, seeds, olives, olive oil, salmon, tuna, dark chocolate, tofu, eggs.
  Bad fats: processed foods, baked goods, fried foods, margarine.
- Lack of **protein** leads to sluggishness, fogginess, anxiety, confusion, fatigue, and depression. Too much protein can result in irritability and depression. Protein is found in fish, chicken, beans, nuts, and seeds.
- Foods that help with **anxiety**: whole grains, beans, bananas, oats, milk, cheese, poultry, soy, nuts, sesame, peanut butter, passionflower, kava. Magnesium is beneficial as well.
- **ADHD** is linked to low levels of dopamine, artificial food dyes, trans fats, carbohydrates, and sugar.
- Foods that help with **cognitive functioning**: antioxidants, flavonoids, vitamins B6, B12, D, and E, choline, copper, iron, calcium, zinc, selenium.
- **Turmeric** helps with Alzheimer's disease and cognitive impairment, depression, stress, insomnia, trauma, and anxiety.
- **Sage** improves memory and attention.
- **Rosemary** improves memory.
- **Peppermint** and cinnamon help with alertness and reduce fatigue.
- Food sensitivities can lead to anxiety, depression, and bipolar disorder. Figure out food allergies and sensitivities by means of the elimination diet or pulse test.

The effects of lifestyle diseases on mental health

Lifestyle diseases are chronic effects of consistently unhealthy food and lifestyle choices in the form of systemic changes in the body, such as in our gut. Our gut influences our entire body, including our brain and mental health. The microbiome, which is the whole of bacteria and microbes living in or on our bodies, impacts the level of stress that we can handle and the way we learn. An unhealthy microbiome appears to affect mood and cognition, leading to disorders like bipolar disorder, Parkinson's disease, and schizophrenia. The use of antibiotics has shown an increase in manic episodes in psychiatric patients. Our standard Western diet, high in saturated fats and sugar, as well as antibiotics and stress seem to possibly cause inflammation in the brain, which again induces psychiatric symptoms. Prenatal stress and cesarean births have shown to affect the infant microbiome.

Prebiotics and probiotics may be a way to support psychiatric treatments[25]. Prebiotics are indigestible carbohydrates or fiber that are fermented in our colon by gut bacteria, reducing levels of cortisol, influencing emotional processes in the brain, and promoting mental flexibility. They can be found in raw onion, garlic, leeks, lentils, Jerusalem artichokes, asparagus, bananas, and dark chocolate[26]. There are many different probiotics with distinct functions, such as improving mood due to their effect on various neurotransmitters, regulating pain and appetite, and reducing inflammation, anxiety, stress, and fear. Natural probiotics are fermented foods including yogurt, sauerkraut, kimchi, and kefir[27]. Eating complex carbohydrates, which are found in dairy, nuts, seeds, legumes, whole grains, fruits, and vegetables, positively affect gut health as well[28].

Schizophrenia often presents with gastrointestinal barrier dysfunction, food sensitivities, inflammation, and metabolic syndrome. Targeting gut issues and inflammation may help to prevent emerging psychotic illness, but findings are contradictory[29].

That said, a healthy gut can only make us feel better. If eating healthy and taking care of our bodies properly benefits our mental health as well, we can only win. Making the choice to live healthier will enhance our overall well-being, and even small improvements need to be considered progress. Sometimes the goal is not fixing but managing the problem at hand.

The rate of autism has increased elevenfold over the last decade, with one out of 166 cases when it used to be 3 out of 10,000[30]. Some researchers believe that there is a link between autism and gut flora. They suggest that ingesting probiotics and fermented foods as well as avoiding dairy products, gluten, corn, and yeast may improve symptoms of autism. Immune system abnormalities, bigger and even swollen brains, and inflammation have been observed in cases of autism[31].

Inflammation, in fact, has been linked to Alzheimer's, autism, fatigue, irritability, and depression. According to Hyman, sources of inflammation are:

- Refined carbohydrates (sugar, white flour products, white rice)
- Foods low in fiber
- High omega-6/omega-3 ratio in our diet and vegetable oils high in omega-6 fatty acids (soybean oil, corn oil, sunflower oil)
- Nutritional deficiencies
- Allergens, toxins, pesticides, and hormones
- Infections, antibiotics, and acid-blocking medication
- Alcohol, caffeine, and steroids
- Constant stress

Reducing red meats and increasing fish, walnuts, whole grains, olive oil, fruits, tomatoes, and green leafy vegetables helps to decrease inflammation. Many spices, such as ginger, chili peppers, black pepper, and turmeric have anti-inflammatory qualities as well.

Stress comes with elevated cortisol, which is a hormone that suppresses the immune system. Omega-3 fatty acids, vitamin C, and black tea may help reduce cortisol levels, while caffeine raises them. Working on lifestyle choices, time management, relationships, work issues, and relaxation techniques helps to relieve stress. It is crucial to also find some joy in daily life. It makes everything we have to do for our well-being much easier and worthwhile. If we feel that time does not permit any joy, we need to identify what we do that prevents us from establishing balance. If finances hinder us from having a good time, we need to rethink what we like to do for fun and find hobbies and activities that don't cost money. We need to learn to think out of the box and become more flexible rather than standing in our own way, focusing on all the things we cannot have. Learning to appreciate what works and being grateful for it is an immense stress relief.

Pesticides appear to have a huge impact on our mental health as well, due to their ability to attack the human nervous system. They have been linked to cognitive deficits, impaired perception and memory, reduced IQs, diminished spatial reasoning and visual processing, ADHD in children, and Parkinson's disease. Brain imaging has shown a thinning of the prefrontal cortex due to pesticides. They may also affect estrogen and testosterone, leading to hormonal changes and impaired sexual functioning and organ development. Similarly, decreased levels of thyroid hormone have possibly been linked to pesticides[32]. Dementia has been linked to high levels of mercury[33], the use of which has been restricted in newer forms of pesticides but was common in earlier versions.

The effects of lifestyle diseases on mental health – *an overview*

- Our **gut** and microbiome influence body and brain.
- **Antibiotics** have shown to negatively affect bipolar disorder.
- Prebiotics and probiotics may support psychiatric treatments. Natural **prebiotics** can be found in raw onion, garlic, leeks, lentils, artichokes, asparagus, bananas, and dark chocolate.
- Natural **probiotics** are fermented foods like yogurt, sauerkraut, kimchi, and kefir.
- **Complex carbohydrates**, such as dairy, nuts, seeds, legumes, whole grain, fruits, and vegetables, positively affect gut health.
- **Autism** seems to improve with probiotics and fermented foods. Avoid dairy, gluten, and corn.
- **Inflammation** has been linked to Alzheimer's disease, fatigue, and depression. Anti-inflammatory qualities are found in fish, walnuts, whole grains, olive oil, fruits, green leafy vegetables, tomatoes, and various spices, such as ginger, chili peppers, black pepper, and turmeric.
- Foods that help with **stress** are foods rich in omega-3s, vitamin C, and black tea. Avoid caffeine. Find joy.
- **Pesticides** have been linked to cognitive deficits, impaired memory, reduced IQs, ADHD, Parkinson's disease, and hormonal changes impairing sexual functioning.

Achieving mental health

There are certainly many factors that play a role in mental health. Diet is only one factor that needs more attention. Other factors are genetics, stress, physical inactivity, thought processes, and environmental impacts. Depression is predicted to be the second biggest cause of disease burden worldwide by 2020, with cardiovascular disease being number one. The more depressed people are, the less likely they are to make healthy choices that lead to improved mental health. Making unhealthy choices worsens their depressed mood, and they find themselves stuck in a vicious cycle.

We need to remember that supplementing one nutrient in isolation will not be sufficient, since in nature nutrients are also consumed in combination and never one at a time. We need to find out which nutrients we are missing and which ones we have too much of. Supplementation, however, is not as effective as adjusting one's diet and eating natural foods[34]. To approach supplementation correctly and avoid harm to our physical health, it is highly recommended to consult a professional rather than experimenting on our own.

Clearly, nutrients work in synergy, they overlap and interact[35]. It is crucial to give our body what it needs, which may differ from person to person. What works for one does not necessarily work for another. Learning to listen to our bodies and keep them healthy by nourishing them properly is as essential as quitting the junk that harms our physical health with empty and possibly toxic calories, creating systemic imbalances and inflammation and causing havoc on a daily basis.

Brains can heal and repair themselves due to brain plasticity. Nutrition, physical exercise, relaxation, and new learning all support new cell formation and healing, while lifestyle choices like watching TV, lack of sleep, drinking sodas, ingesting excessive amount of caffeine and alcohol, GMO products, fights and arguments, and talking on our cell phones too much hurt our brain[36]. Therefore, picking some of the suggestions from each chapter of this book and applying them consistently, will provide a broad approach to personal healing, physical, emotional, mental, and spiritual, and increased happiness.

Achieving mental health – *an overview*

- Many factors determine our mental health: diet, genetics, stress, physical activity level, thought processes, and environment.
- All these factors need to be addressed on a constant basis.
- Brains can heal, but we need to support them to do so.
- Live healthy and avoid the junk.

How to think what you want to think

Ninety percent of illnesses are caused, or worsened, by stress and negative thoughts which influence how we feel, because our mind influences our body[37]. Therefore, our thoughts in combination with bad nutrition can propel us into a downward spiral of physical and mental disease. Consistent and comprehensive changes in how we live our daily lives are often needed to find our way back to health and maintain it.

We need to learn to cope with our negative thoughts before we can detach from them. We need to acknowledge, accept, and replace them with healthier and more positive thoughts that have the capability to move us forward. This way we stop letting thoughts and feelings control us and reclaim control over them instead[38].

Thought stopping and replacing

One of the first tools I teach my clients is to stop what they are thinking. To most, this sounds impossible, but it really is not. It can be very hard because this technique needs dedication, commitment, and consistency. The problem with negative thoughts is that due to their habitual nature, we indoctrinate ourselves with negative messages. We keep telling ourselves what we are afraid of, what is not working, what is bad, and what hurts over and over again; we start feeling hopelessness, helplessness, despair, loss, and fear. We feel that nothing can ever change or get better, which in this mindset is somewhat true because even if things improved we would not be able to notice them since our focus is on failing, and we do not allow ourselves to see anything that does not fit our expectations, negative or positive. When we have negative thoughts, we feel awful, which negatively affects our thoughts even more. When thoughts get worse, the feelings do too. As our feelings get worse, so do our thought processes. This is a spiral that is progressive and a challenge to escape from. But it can be done. These are OUR thoughts. These are OUR feelings. We can reclaim control over them, we are the boss. If we are not, we need to make sure we change that.

The first step in learning to stop our negative thoughts and control them is noticing them. We need to be completely aware of what is going on in our heads. When my clients start noticing their thoughts, and I mean TRULY noticing them, they are stunned at the realization of how negative they are. Once we notice these thoughts, we need to acknowledge them. They are part of our truth and relevant at the time. However, that is where the tricky part starts: we must push them away next, negate them, and argue with them. We need to tell ourselves how these thoughts are wrong, even if it's only one part of that thought that we don't agree with a hundred percent. For example, instead of "everything is bad" we can rather think: "Well, it feels like everything is bad. But it's only this one situation that troubles me right now." We must consciously respond to our negative thoughts and fight them within our own heads, even if we are afraid that this could make us look a little looney. Thoughts can drive us crazy enough anyway, so why not beat them at their own game?

Once we notice our negative thoughts, acknowledge them, negate them, and change them up, we have to replace them with other thoughts that work for us at that moment. If we only push thoughts away but do not replace them, they will come right back into our heads. In the above example, we could follow up with: "This situation IS bad, but I've got this," or "I can do this, I don't know how, but I can," or simply "I am ok anyway, I am fine." Rather than having negative thoughts dominate our heads, we can choose more positive ones. "I am ok" is the easiest one to come up with, and basically, we can go through our entire day telling ourselves that until we start feeling a little better. As I tell my clients all the time, thoughts come first, feelings follow. If our thoughts are negative, so are our feelings. If our thoughts change to being more positive, we will gradually feel more hopeful also.

This exercise sounds simple enough, but impossible at the same time, because when negative thoughts keep coming into our minds every hour, every minute, or even every second, we must keep noticing, acknowledging, pushing away, and replacing them every single time. This is as tedious as it sounds, but it is also such a necessary and effective tool. If we have to do it 50 times a minute this week, it may be 30 times a minute next week, and 10 times a minute the following week. What that means is that our negative thoughts will reduce slowly and gradually in number and intensity, as long as we keep using this skill consistently over a period of time. In a month or two we may have more peace in our minds, more calm moments, and fewer intrusive thoughts than we used to have before. If this sounds like it takes too much time, we need to remember how long we have already suffered due to our internal mental torture and how many years are still to come, years that would be much easier and more enjoyable for us if we finally allowed ourselves to be happier. Breaking habits, even if they are of the mental kind – or maybe especially because they are of the mental kind – is always hard work and takes time, dedication, and patience.

We need to keep in mind, though, that our brain never forgets these thoughts that used to put us down, that made us want to give up, and that made our lives hell. At the same time, we need to stop our brain from reverting back to using them during crises or difficult situations. These are the times when dysfunctional thoughts are more likely to emerge again. If they do, that does not mean our thought changing efforts did not work, it simply means that we have to apply them again, with the difference that now we at least know how. We will notice that this time, taking control of our thought processes is much easier to accomplish. We manage to conquer our negative thoughts as they come up, one after the other, they go away much faster than before, and are not as intense as they used to be. Negative thoughts may come up intermittently, but what matters is what we do with them and how we react to them. That very reaction is what we need to be in control of.

Positive self-affirmations

Stopping and replacing our negative thoughts is very similar to the coping skill I am going to discuss next: positive self-talk. When we replace our dysfunctional thoughts, we need to find not only positive, but also for us acceptable messages that are better than our original thoughts. It can be one simple statement that we tell ourselves over and over again, all day long, like "I am ok", or it can be different ones that we adjust to the specific situation we find ourselves in. These messages are limitless, but here are a few examples:

- I am ok.
- I am fine.
- I've got this.
- I can do this.
- I choose to do this.
- I am working on it.
- Everything is fine.
- Relax.
- Peace.
- Love.
- It is getting better, one day at a time.

> I choose to believe that things are getting better.
> I choose to love myself today – just today, just a little bit.

Of course, everybody needs to use statements that work for them and their specific situation. We can drive our car and think "I'm great" all the way until we reach our destination to keep us from focusing on negative thoughts. We can tell ourselves "relax, relax, relax" over and over again, and eventually we feel more relaxed because we allow ourselves to, based on the words spoken in our minds.

In the 1990s, Masaru Emoto did astounding experiments with water that illustrate the impact of our spoken words on our entire body system and consequently on that of others as well. He froze two glasses of water and put each of them on a piece of paper, one of them had the word "love" written on it, the other one the word "hate". When he looked at the frozen water under the microscope, the water in the glass with the word "love" underneath had frozen in the form of beautiful water crystals, as expected. However, the water in the glass with the word "hate" underneath was entirely out of shape and irregular. There were no beautiful water crystals to be detected. This experiment was replicated with words spoken to glasses filled with water with the same results. If we consider that two thirds of our bodies are water and that the energy of words affects water in general, we can only imagine how negative talk can affect our entire system and everyone else around us.

"Words are things," we hear that phrase all the time. They affect our mental and emotional health, and Emoto's experiments clearly demonstrate how powerful they are and how they resonate in our bodies. On a slightly different note, self-fulfilling prophecies do exist. If we focus on a certain outcome it is likely that it is going to happen that way, because subconsciously we are taking steps to make it happen. Similarly, if we focus on our fears, we are subconsciously working on the outcome we are most afraid of and want to avoid. We cannot tell our brain what we do not want and expect good results. Our brain ignores the word "not" and will work exactly towards what we don't want. So, telling ourselves "I don't want to cry" will most likely not work, because our brain would only focus on the word "cry", and eventually we lose self-control and cry anyway. Self-statements need to be positive, in this example we can say "I am calm" instead of using the word "cry", then our brain can work towards being calm, and crying would not even be a thought. Literally.

Egocentric thought patterns

Based on the last section, it becomes obvious how crucial it is to avoid self-blame and self-pity. Both are dysfunctional thought processes and fill our brain with negative words and feelings. Putting ourselves down and calling ourselves "bad" and "useless" will have effects on our thinking and feeling, similar to feeling sorry for ourselves and seeing everyone else as bad, useless, and messing up. In both instances, we feel that we are not okay, and we blame someone, either ourselves or others. We feel powerless to change anything, and we are unhappy with our lives and the world.

When we tend to blame ourselves, we need to learn to acknowledge that we matter. We need to allow ourselves to make mistakes and give ourselves a chance to correct them. We need to learn self-forgiveness, to get out of the past, and live in the present moment.

Similarly, when we tend to feel sorry for ourselves, we not only need to acknowledge that WE matter, but we also need to acknowledge that OTHERS matter, too. We need to accept that not everything is going to go our way, allow others to make mistakes, and give them a chance to correct them also. We need to learn to forgive others, remove ourselves from the past, and move into the present moment, just like it is the case with self-blame.

Both self-blame and self-pity are egocentric thought patterns that are manipulative and controlling. However, if we, in fact, find ourselves in situations where others "make us feel guilty" or where others keep walking over us, we need to work through our relationships and self-value, learn to set boundaries, and make choices accordingly to protect ourselves from being manipulated going forward. These processes can best be tackled in psychotherapy one step at a time, exploring where our beliefs and resulting choices stem from. Until then, the word "no" can go a long way.

Related to self-pity is the tendency to take things personally. This is another egocentric thought pattern that gives us the feeling that others do things to hurt us deliberately. If we think about this a little more closely, we would have to be very important to make others go out of their way to talk about us, think about us, or hurt us deliberately all the time. When certain situations feel personal, it is good practice to clarify that by expressing to the other person how their actions and words feel to us. This gives them the opportunity to clear up misunderstandings or apologize for thoughtless choices.

Carrying grudges harms relationships and hurts ourselves most due to the resulting resentment that can literally make our bodies and minds sick. We can learn to cope with grudges and resentment in psychotherapy by working on acceptance, self-value, and letting go of the past. However, as stated above, if there is no misunderstanding and we do have people around us who like lashing out at us and probably everyone else as well for that matter, or who are frequently condescending and demeaning, we need to rethink our relationship with them, strengthen our boundaries, and make choices to protect ourselves from their negativity rather than continuing these hurtful, imbalanced, and destructive relationships.

Anxiety-provoking thought patterns

Another very common and stressful negative thought pattern is thinking "what if." What-ifs are only looking for bad things to happen and are the cause of a lot of anxiety and fear. What-ifs may be based on negative experiences in the past and see the future as more struggles and pain in the making. They are mostly detached from what is actually going on in our present and can leave us lost, helpless, defeated, and scared without anything bad ever happening. What-ifs are not a way of preparing for eventualities, they are simply worries. To constructively prepare for what the future may bring, our thoughts must be neutral and matter-of-fact instead of emotionally charged with the energy of fear. Also, the verbiage is different between what-ifs and preparation. Preparation sounds like: "If this is going to happen, I am going to do that." What-ifs, on the other hand, do not offer a solution: "What if this is going to happen?" Thinking this way is giving up our power to resolve any situation and leaves our focus on the problem itself. Preparing for a potentially problematic situation parallels the thought stopping and replacing technique mentioned above and teaches our brain to habitually look for solutions rather than getting stuck on our fears. It gives us the feeling that we can actually do something about the issue at hand.

A lot of stress results from unrealistic expectations of ourselves and others. Our expectations of ourselves may not even be ours but may have originated from parents, spouses, children, or friends. At times we accept them and take them on as our own, but fail to meet them because in truth, they have nothing to do with our goals and direction in life. We believe that we "should" be able to accomplish what is expected of us, but at the same time don't seem to have the drive to follow through, and we criticize ourselves then for our constant procrastination.

On a side note, the word "should" needs to be avoided at all times. Either we do or we don't, or we can or cannot. The word "should" puts a lot of pressure on us to accomplish something while implying that it may not even be possible or desirable. I am certain that if we really want to do something, we can follow through. If we procrastinate, there is one reason or another why we seem to lack motivation, and it is crucial to look for these reasons.

Similarly, other people's expectations of us or our expectations of others can cause the same amount of stress. Other people's random expectations can put immense pressure on us and we may feel criticized when clearly it is not up to them what we choose to do, and vice versa. Expectations can be like commands that we are told to follow, and they can be very unhealthy. That said, we need to distinguish between random expectations and expectations based on previous arrangements.

If we need a random favor or a service from someone, an expectation is not the approach to take. We can simply ask for what we need. Of course, if the answer is "no", we need to accept that, too. If we don't, our expectations falsely lead to hurt, disappointment, and even anger based on feelings of entitlement. Expecting others to always do as we ask is selfish and disregards the other person's right to choose. If we feel that we give whenever possible, but we don't get anything back because the answer always seems to be "no", there is an imbalance in the relationship and we again need to rethink if this relationship is a healthy one. In a functioning relationship, there is a give and take, both sides can ask for what they need and want, and there will be some "yes's" and some "no's", and this needs to be perfectly fine. However, we also need to accept that some people are merely takers, and we have to figure out what we are ready to do about setting healthy boundaries. One thing is certain: we cannot change THEM. In the opposite case that the other person always helps us out without fail, we can consider ourselves lucky. At the same time, we must not expect them to continue to do so every single time we ask a favor of them, only because they started off that way. Life happens, and so do "no's", and we need to accept them as they come.

Expectations based on arrangements, previous deals, promises, or certain rules that have been communicated to and agreed upon by all parties involved are a different story altogether. There we can expect the other party to follow through, otherwise the arrangement would not mean anything. If that does not happen, there can be consequences or even a dissolution of the deal or relationship. The crucial point is that there has been clear communication and an agreement about what can be expected. The situation is transparent and not based on random wants and needs that others cannot possibly know about or may be unable to help with at this specific time. Not following through on previous arrangements is a sign of irresponsibility and unreliability.

If others do not follow through with a previously made deal, our negative emotional response may be justifiable, but still not healthy, due to the disrespect that their choices entail. Their defensiveness, justification of their lack of commitment, and inconsiderate behavior cause us even more stress that we have to learn to cope with to avoid negative reactions.

The bottom line is, we need to avoid random expectations, communicate properly, ask for what we need, and stick to agreements to the best of our ability. At the same time, we cannot expect others to do the same, ever. But we can at least ask them to try.

Assumptions are another source of stress. They lead to misunderstandings based on believing that others know what we need, want, feel, and think, as well as the expectation that others will make sure to meet our needs. Both these beliefs and expectations are unrealistic and need to be communicated to avoid misunderstandings and disappointments.

To assume that our loved ones will hurt us in ways others have hurt us before is not only unfair to the people in our present who may be entirely different from people in our past, but it also hurts us by keeping us afraid, stuck in the past, and detached. There is clearly a lack of communication involved with assumptions that can end in hurt feelings and anger. People cannot read our minds or pick up on our feelings that accurately. When we sulk, they often have no clue why we do, even though we assume they "should" know exactly what the problem is. As stated before, there is no "should", either they do or they don't. Rather than waiting for them to beg us to tell them what the problem is so they can do something to help us, we could simply communicate our feelings and needs. Assumptions hurt both sides, one side feels misunderstood and that they don't matter, and the other feels pressured and helpless. Nobody wins.

Having explored these common examples of negative thought patterns, it is obvious that all of these can cause us a lot of stress and are usually pervasive and habitual. As mentioned above, stress means more cortisol in our system, and more cortisol may lead to heart disease, anxiety, depression, dementia, hypertension, and gastrointestinal disorders. Constantly elevated stress hormones affect our immune system, mood, feelings of well-being and happiness, memory, and personal growth. Our thoughts clearly affect our body and mind, and we need to work on our thought processes every day.

Acceptance and gratitude

Working on acceptance is a big step towards happiness. We need to accept what happened and what we cannot change, no matter if we like it or not. We also need to accept who we are and where we are in our lives right now. At the same time, we need to accept others for who they are and where they are in their lives right now, too. We cannot change any of that this very moment, but we can continuously work on improving our lives. We need to stop fighting what was, accept what is, and adjust as needed to move forward to a promising future. Acceptance reduces the perception of stress because there is no more fighting.

Acceptance allows us to be thankful for what is and for how far we have already come. We can see life as a huge lesson and as an adventure that is getting us closer to our goals and potential. We need to be grateful for what we have in life, for who we are today, and the people in our lives. We can also choose to be grateful for what was and what it helped us become because every experience in life, no matter how hard it might have been living through it, has the potential to make us a bigger person, if we allow it. At least we can be grateful that tough times are over and we made it through. If we experience ongoing struggles, we can be grateful for our strength to be hanging in there still and the support we have that keeps us going. With gratitude we find peace and love. With love we achieve healing and joy in life.

Another technique that brings love, acceptance, peace, and joy is mindfulness, which has been discussed previously. With mindfulness, focusing on our five senses, we learn to turn off our thoughts and rest our brain. We learn to be still and in the present moment. In the present moment we find our true selves because that is the only place where we can be, the past is gone and the future does not exist yet. A daily practice of mindfulness will make us stronger and more connected to our Higher Selves and Higher Power.

When we really feel lost and don't know any more what to do next, we can brainstorm with family or friends, figuring out together what is going on in our mind and where to go from here. Asking for help and support is always a good tool to have, therefore, we need to take care of and treasure our support system. At times, the perspectives of our loved ones are the best starting point to tackle another mental challenge. It can give us hope and boost us towards a manageable place where we can regroup and from which we can take our next constructive steps forward.

Forgiveness

Forgiveness is key, it helps us to let go of hurt and anger, it reduces stress and depressed mood. It fosters hope, optimism, and compassion, as well as perceived physical well-being as it positively affects tension and pain, stomach issues, sleep, and energy levels[39]. It is not about letting the other person off the hook, but about setting ourselves free. If we feel the need to do so, we can even choose to let go of any ties to them. Forgiving others does not mean that we have to let them back into our lives if we have no desire to do so or if the relationship has been merely toxic in the first place. At the same time, we don't have to sever relationships in order to forgive, as long as positive regard, respect, and trust are still given.

Holding grudges usually does not hurt anyone else but ourselves. Forgiveness helps us to let go of any expectations and facilitates acceptance and peace. In order to forgive, we must acknowledge our pain, accept what we cannot change, decide to move forward, and possibly send love and light to the person that has caused our heartache or agony. If we manage to be grateful for what we have learned, being free of the pain, having grown, and having found love in our hearts again at the end of the forgiveness process, we allow ourselves to finally find happiness in ourselves, which benefits our physical and mental health, attitude, and relationships in our lives.

To keep our cognitive functioning optimal and be able to continue working on our thought processes as we progress in years, we need to do mental exercises, such as crossword puzzles, sudokus, math exercises, memorizing, participating in game shows actively when watching TV, and challenging our thoughts and memory on a regular basis. Trust the saying: when we don't use it, we lose it. It applies to our brain health and functioning as we get older as well. If we get lazy and stop using our cognitive abilities, our brain will slow down. Just like with our physical health, if we stop exercising and using our muscles, we lose them, too.

Finally, whatever we do, we need to do the best we can. When we know that we always give our best, we will not get upset whenever anyone criticizes us and says that we are not doing enough because we know better than that. We need to trust ourselves, trust what we know, do the best we can, and we will free ourselves from other people's judgments. This concept, as well as the importance to choose the words we speak and think well, avoid assumptions and expectations, and not take anything personally, follows Don Miguel Ruiz's ideas shared in his wonderful book *The Four Agreements.*

How to think what you want to think – an overview

- Control your thoughts: notice, acknowledge, push away, replace.
- Our brains never forget. That doesn't mean we cannot move forward.
- Watch your self-talk, make it positive.
- Focus on what you want, not on what you don't want.
- Avoid self-blame and self-pity as they are negative and self-defeating.
- Don't take things personally, it's not always about you.
- Avoid what-ifs, they only cause anxiety and fear. Look for solutions.
- Avoid expectations. If you need something, ask for it.
- Avoid assumptions. Communicate and avoid the guessing game.
- Dysfunctional thought processes cause stress.
- Acceptance leads to happiness.
- Gratitude leads to peace, love, healing, and joy.
- Forgiveness leads to physical and mental health.
- Mindfulness helps you to stay in the present moment.
- Treasure your support system.
- Keep training your brain.
- Always do the best you can.

How to support your kids

It is crucial to teach children how to control their thoughts and how not only to accept other people's perspectives but also develop their own. They need to learn to define their own worldview, change what they can change, but also accept what they cannot change, as it is so nicely worded in the well-known serenity prayer. It requires coping skills to accept something we do not agree with, without having to change our own perspective that is our personal truth. The greatest challenge with helping children to define their own worldview is that many adults have not learned to do this yet themselves because they were also taught to follow societal standards and adjust their thinking to their environment. Kids need to find the middle between being a rebel and losing themselves in dictated norms, live according to their own ideas and values without disregarding common rules and without hurting anyone else nor themselves, and develop personal freedom to be the individual they long to be. This is not made easy due to societal pressures, but it can be done. Once adults make some progress in this direction, children will be able to find their own individuality much more easily as well.

Like adults, children need to learn the following skills:

- Identify what is going on in their minds and push away and change their negative thoughts

- Work on positive self-talk and carefully choosing the words they speak to themselves and others
- Replace self-doubt and self-criticism with self-affirmations
- Be in the present and plan ahead rather than focus on the past and worry about what could happen in the future
- Protect themselves from others, their judgments, and gossip

Kids will not know to do any of these and how to start unless we teach them, but they will benefit from these skills for the rest of their lives.

We need to teach children to communicate properly, to ask for what they need, and to avoid making expectations and assumptions. They need to learn to ask appropriate questions to clarify what other people mean and think. Proper communication prevents unnecessary misunderstandings, improves relationships, and allows everybody to express their standpoint and how they feel about certain things and situations without judgment. When proper communication is established in families, it is much easier to talk to children about their personal challenges as well. They need to feel comfortable talking to parents, knowing that they will not be judged or ridiculed because their feelings matter and that they have a voice and the permission to use it. They need to know that they are okay the way they are, and it clearly starts within the family.

If parents disagree with their kids having a different perspective, or if they think that children don't need a voice yet because in their opinion they don't know enough of life so far, children cannot develop self-confidence and a positive self-image. These parents foster dependence, lack of individuality, lack of freedom of thoughts, lack of self-esteem, and a lot of anger, all challenges we do not want children to have to struggle with because we know far too well how it feels to be in this place. Parents need to allow them to grow into independent and free-thinking, but still caring and considerate, young adults rather than hold them back and mold them to their own liking. Children will develop a caring and considerate attitude if parents model it for them. Parents also need to refrain from spoiling and enabling them too much as they grow up, like letting them get away with avoiding their responsibilities or handing them everything they need or want rather than teaching them how to help themselves, because parents think they are too young to be taught how to be responsible or independent. Parents need to support their kids' professional and personal interests and show them that they matter, even if they make mistakes. That's one of the greatest gifts parents can give them.

One final thought about parenting: Whenever children come up and follow through with ideas that don't hurt them or anyone else, even if parents do not agree with or support these ideas, there is no need to stop them from trying or tell them "I told you so" if things do not work out. Parents can offer guidance, but kids still need to be encouraged to venture out and make their own experiences. They need to be congratulated for their courage and supported when they need help. It's ok to be proud of our offspring as they struggle to become their own. If parents catch themselves holding their kids back, it's probably due to their own fear of failure and sticking out of the crowd.

How to support your kids – *an overview*

- Teach your children to control their thoughts.
- Teach your children to accept other people's perspectives.
- Teach your children that there are things they cannot change and they need to accept. They don't have to like them.
- Teach your children to watch the words they speak.
- Teach your children to be in the present moment.
- Teach your children how to protect themselves from other people's judgment and gossip.
- Teach your children how to communicate.
- Allow your children to develop their own perspectives and worldview.
- Allow your children to be individuals.
- Give your children a voice that matters.
- "I told you so" is a no-no.
- Be proud of your children and their courage to venture out.

CHAPTER 6

The spiritual body

Spirituality is challenging to discuss because it is understood in so many different ways. For some it is religion, for others it does not have anything to do with religion but is merely their connection with their Higher Power. Some people only believe in science and demand evidence to prove that there is something out there that supposedly has such immense power and control. Others again just have a knowing that there is a power that guides their every move. Some people share their beliefs openly, and for others it is an entirely personal relationship that they pursue strictly in private. Then there are people who search for whatever that Higher Power may be and for a definition of what they cannot see and are unsure of whether they even feel. There is a lot of judgment, expectations, and fear among people about faith, beliefs, religion, and spirituality. This book does not suggest a specific religious or spiritual direction because there is none that works for everybody. It also does not discuss what is right or wrong because there simply is no absolute right or wrong. Spirituality is individualistic as every other concept touched on above. Spirituality is whatever we make of it, and it has the importance and power that we give it.

Spirituality influences people greatly in terms of their identity and how they interact with their environment[1]. If God is loving, we want to love. If God is giving, we want to give. If God is healing, we want to heal. If God is accepting, we want to accept. If God is forgiving, we want to forgive. If we followed the examples of godly actions and behavior described in many religious books, there would be so much more peace, love, joy, acceptance, and togetherness in our world, and much less judgment, fear, envy, and criticism. We do not just want to read about what we need to do to be the best we can be, where to find God or our Higher Power, and the consequences of our actions that will only put fear in us. We need to start applying all these wonderful concepts we read about and discuss with others who share our interests and beliefs. Being spiritual means bettering ourselves every day, growing, becoming a greater person, and moving towards our goal of what perfect love means to us - love for God, Nature, our Higher Power, Higher Self, Science, others, and ourselves.

To be able to feel truly connected to God, we need to first feel connected to ourselves and pay attention to what is happening in our hearts, no matter if there is joy or pain. We need to acknowledge, feel, accept, and use what we find for our personal growth, so we can move forward. Silence, solitude, and avoiding any distractions are ideal premises to start listening to ourselves, learning to be comfortable on our own, and quieting our mind and body. There is power in stillness[2]. Mindfulness gives you stillness, and from mindfulness we can progress to meditation. If we manage to be still we may have stopped running away from our difficulties, hurts, and fears. As long as we are running, we cannot be still, and as long as we are not still, we keep running. We need to work through our emotional and mental challenges to find peace and quietness in our minds, and live and feel our connection with God, Higher Power, Nature, Higher Self, or Science. In stillness, our spiritual body overlaps with our physical, emotional, and mental bodies. One does not exist without the other, all four bodies are one.

Spirituality has a lot to do with finding meaning and purpose in life which come along with self-awareness, a sense of identity, change, and growth. Even atheism can be considered a form of spirituality because meaning is derived from nature and personal experiences[3]. Spirituality can also mean being in tune with our own spirit or soul. Without meaning and purpose we feel lost and keep searching. This may lead to a feeling of anxiety because our spirit or soul is looking for answers that we have not found yet, and anxiety keeps us looking for these answers. However, if we are spiritually unaware, we often do not know what we are seeking or what we are missing, we only feel emptiness. If we are not in tune with our spirit or soul, we don't know that anxiety is its way of crying out to get us back onto our path to do what we are meant to do. This may be serving, helping, starting something new, spreading love, learning to forgive, leading by example, or supporting a loved one to reach their goals. There are endless possibilities of what we may want or need to accomplish in our lifetime. Even if we are currently unaware of what our purpose may be, giving it some thought, healing old pain, finding joy in the present moment, and a meaningful spiritual connection usually lead to some answers, which can be apparent or totally unexpected. We can spread love in our daily lives and touch many people this way. Not all of us will be a Mother Teresa, a hero, a martyr, or a saint. Many of us may never know how much we have done for others and will still feel accomplished by simply living love in the here and now. Others will find their peace and divine connection in nature and live true to themselves without touching many other lives, but they experience fulfillment nevertheless by living their own spiritual truth, true to their own personal values.

Whatever spirituality is or is not, we need to find out what meaning it has in our own lives. Do we find our connection to our Higher Power in church, nature, our home, our pets, family, friends, or ourselves? All these possibilities and many more are valid and acceptable. Whatever works for us needs to be acknowledged and pursued. We need to trust in ourselves to find our truth, and Spirit always finds a way to reach us whenever we are ready to listen.

When individuals pursue spirituality in a manner that is different from the majority's understanding they are often met with judgment. But if God is love and love is acceptance and embracing others no matter what, we have no right to judge them and where they are in their life right now, even if our faith takes us into a different direction. We need to love unconditionally and without judgment; we can share our thoughts if invited to do so and keep them to ourselves if not. We need to treat everyone like we would our family and friends in any other matter and the way we want to be treated ourselves: we love and accept them unconditionally and don't try to "fix" them. We simply can never ever "fix" anyone, not only because our mold may not fit anyone else in the first place, but also because everyone needs to find their own path themselves and pursue their personal goals, whatever they are. We can only stand by with love and support, and avoid judgment, criticism, and unwanted advice.

Spirituality is a huge component in our lives, even if we are not aware of it or if we don't even believe that there is anything out there that is bigger than us. Without this connection we often feel lost, our lives may feel meaningless, and we may feel intense anxiety and loneliness that we do not understand. It is a well-known concept in the world of addiction that as people sink deeper and deeper into this illness, they lose God. As addicts recover, they report the feeling of having had a huge hole in their core, which their lost spirituality had left behind. That hole is being filled as they recover and find their Higher Power again. It is open for discussion whether it is these feelings of being lost, having no meaning, anxiety, loneliness, and emptiness that make us create a sort of spirituality in our minds to cope with these painful emotions or if there, indeed, is a Higher Power that makes us feel whole when we find it.

The spiritual body – an overview

- Spirituality is individualistic. Some have found their ways, some are searching.
- We need to learn to accept where we are and where others are without judgment.
- Live your spiritual values daily.
- Learn to understand yourself, accept what you find, and move forward.
- Learn to be still and find your spiritual connection.
- Find your personal meaning and purpose in life and live it.
- Love and accept unconditionally.
- We cannot fix anyone, we can only work on ourselves.
- Without spirituality we may feel lost, meaningless, anxious, lonely, or empty.

How to live your spirituality

Meditation has shown to increase brain size while improving mood and cognitive functions. For many, however, meditation seems to be a difficult task to tackle. This may be due to our hectic lifestyles and busy schedules. Another reason may be, as mentioned above, that we keep running away from feelings and thoughts that we are not ready to face or process, so we avoid being still. When we are still, thoughts and feelings catch up with us. For some, processing feelings and thoughts from the past, accepting and being in the present moment, creating a life that we really want, and building our future can best be achieved with professional help. Once we have worked through "old stuff" and made changes for a happier and more exciting "here and now", we can start tackling the meditation challenge. From my experience, this is best started off with practicing mindfulness because we can use our senses to keep our minds anchored and stop our thoughts from wandering. Our brains are not used to being still, so we have to inch our way towards stillness. By focusing on what we see, hear, smell, taste, and feel we direct our thoughts to our present moment and away from past hurts and future worries. Our mind may not be entirely still, but at least it is here with us. As we accomplish that, our body is going to slow down and relax. From there we can practice finding even more stillness, gradually reducing the sensations we are focusing on until we are able to concentrate on our breathing or heartbeat only. Eventually we will be able to empty our minds completely and master meditation.

When we practice love, we are being spiritual. Let's love ourselves, love others, love life, love our house, and love our job. Let's be grateful for what is working in our life, embrace the challenges that help us grow, and try to make them work for us. Rather than focusing on what is not working and what makes our life so hard, let's enjoy the things that are good, people in our life, a moment in our backyard or on the balcony of our apartment, our fresh sheets in our bed, a cup of tea while listening to nice music, a walk through our neighborhood, a sunrise or sunset, and let's appreciate a moment of joy and happiness. When we focus on joy and happiness, we create another moment of mindfulness, being present in the here and now, which can give us a feeling of peace. The more joy and happiness we feel, the more peace we experience, because we stop fighting everything in our life that we cannot change at this very moment, if at all. Complaining does not accomplish anything, it only leads to frustration. Sometimes we have to make profound changes in our own lives, because our environment may never improve.

When we struggle in daily life and feel like nothing is working, helping others in need may give us a feeling of accomplishment and purpose and may make us realize that there are people who are more in need than we are. We may learn from them how to ask for help, accept help, manage when we have very little, or find joy in small things. When we give, we receive. Sometimes we help others, and we find that we are being helped, too. Or we offer our help, and we get a sense of doing good and improved self-value. Improved self-value helps us to set healthier boundaries and not let people walk over us. When we stop allowing people to hurt us, we feel happier, and a new force will come into motion that may propel us forward without us even realizing.

When we have questions about spirituality, what is right and wrong, or what we need to do next, it can help to just ask these questions before we go to bed, matter-of-factly and with confidence and gratitude that the answers will come. If we trust to receive answers to our questions, we may indeed get them. This can happen in various ways, such as dreaming about it, seeing a TV show where this specific matter is addressed, seeing a billboard that gives us an answer of some sort, a friend telling us something entirely unrelated that still fits our questions, or a line in a book that we are reading. The answers are out there. By focusing on finding them, rather than feeling helpless, we sharpen our awareness and attention, so we notice things that we otherwise wouldn't. It sounds unreal, but it seems to work without fail because we are actually connecting to our Higher Power or Higher Self, and there is no telling what is possible after we start establishing and relying on this connection once and for all.

Of course, one of the most common ways of living our spirituality is connecting with others of the same faith in a church or spiritual community. Meeting, praying, connecting, sharing, discussing, and focusing on our love for God gives many a sense of belonging and a lot of strength. It helps us to live and deepen our faith and feel like an integral part of a community that supports us through good and not so good times. It is crucial to find a community that fits our personality, where we feel at home and accepted, and where we manage to just be and celebrate. Sometimes this place is in our immediate neighborhood and the one we grew up in, sometimes it may be an entirely new place with entirely different people who make us feel that we belong. Whichever way it is, again, there is no right or wrong. We need to be where we feel the best, the strongest, the happiest, and the truest.

Finally, hobbies like walking, riding a bike, hiking, mountain climbing, and swimming may be meditative for some and may help to connect with our Higher Power. Being present in nature or spending time with animals can be spiritually uplifting, so can music and arts – dancing, singing, playing an instrument, painting, drawing, writing, coloring, and so much more. Creativity and spirituality seem to go hand in hand, and being engaged in one also brings us closer to the other.

Spirituality is very individualistic. We need to do whatever works best for us personally, even if we don't know anyone else who approaches life the same way.

This is only about us and our faith and not about anyone else. Spirituality is a very personal matter, so is our entire life.

How to live your spirituality – an overview

- Work through old pain and worries about the future.
- Start with mindfulness and work your way up to meditation.
- Practice love every day.
- Enjoy and be grateful for what you have.
- Keep your focus on what is good and work on the rest.
- Stop complaining about what you cannot change.
- Help others who are worse off than you.
- Set healthy boundaries.
- Ask your questions and be grateful for the answers that are coming your way.
- A church or spiritual community can be an awesome support system.
- Hobbies, nature, animals, music, and arts can enhance our spirituality.
- Be creative.
- Spirituality is a personal matter.

How to support your kids

Sharing our beliefs and faith with our children opens the conversation about spirituality. They can listen and practice what parents introduce to them, and some will continue on that path, but others may change things up a bit and explore other types of spirituality. That is where conflict can originate. Reading up on and exploring what other cultures live and believe in is mind opening, but many people seem to feel threatened when their children venture out in that manner. Forcing them into a specific faith and stopping them from learning is limiting. They may be curious and explore other avenues, but that does not mean they will distance themselves from what they know, it may even strengthen their relationship to the community they have been a part of. As with sexuality and drugs, talking to them openly about spirituality and religions gives them the opportunity to make educated choices rather than being curious about something that appears to be a secret, which becomes tempting and may be considered worth pursuing for that reason alone. Similarly, force and warnings usually lead to the opposite reaction that we want to elicit. If there is no secret, there is nothing hidden to uncover, just other perspectives to see. If there is no force, there is no reason to rebel. Looking at things this way may help us to conquer our fear that our kids may go down the wrong path.

Letting children be part of our own spiritual routine shows them what works for us and why it does. Taking them to church with us teaches them ways of connecting with God or a Higher Power, how to worship and pray, and how a spiritual community works. Saying prayers at home at the dinner table together, or meditating with our children when putting them to bed keeps spirituality and faith present in our daily routines. This is another gift we can give them, the gift of the connection with a loving God or energy that they can always resort to in times of need or simply show gratitude to. It teaches trust and love, but also humility and modesty.

Meditating with our children is also a gift that is worth giving. Meditation is a way of living, just like church, prayers at the dinner table, and prayers at bedtime. There are so many benefits in meditation for our physical, emotional, mental, and spiritual health, and not teaching our children meditation, or mindfulness for that matter, would deny them one of the greatest coping skills that they can possibly learn. Meditating together is incredibly powerful and connecting, it will enhance our relationship with our children and increase trust, especially if we initiate this routine in early childhood. Relaxation benefits our entire system, it is calming and destressing. We also learn to focus better, which benefits us at school and work and helps us to make decisions. Meditating as a family strengthens our mood, state of mind, relationships, communication, and spiritual life.

How to support your kids – *an overview*

- Allow children to learn and explore other religions and types of spirituality.
- Discuss with them openly what they are finding.
- Avoid secrets and force, they come from fear.
- Church, prayers at home, and open conversations about God bring spirituality into our children's daily lives.
- Meditate with your kids, starting early in their lives.

CHAPTER 7

Self-care in action

Reading a book full of suggestions and ideas that can become part of our personal self-care does not mean that putting these into action is going to be easy. Rather on the contrary, it can be overwhelming and leave the reader wondering where to start. Usually we feel that there is no time left in our busy schedules to implement any self-care, even though it would leave us more energized and therefore enable us to practice better time management. When we sleep and rest more, our brain works better and we can accomplish more in less time, which frees up more time for our self-care and enjoyment. We simply need to get started and allow ourselves to experience subtle changes that will make continuing on this route worth it.

The following diagram shows how we interact with our environment on a physical, emotional, mental, and spiritual level, how we can benefit from our immediate surrounding, but also how we need to set boundaries in all areas of our life. The center circle represents us when we take care of ourselves and names ways how we can contribute to relationships in our lives. The six sections around the circle depict the kind of environments we have in life: Love relationships, family, friends, work, community, and leisure. Each of them is subdivided into two parts: the one closer to us includes how we can benefit from each environment, while the outer one lists possible stressors we may encounter. Wherever we go in life, we can have positive and negative experiences. The lines in-between these parts symbolize the boundaries we need to set in each environment to protect us from negative impacts and stress. The physical level is mainly present in leisure, the emotional and mental aspects are part of each section, while spirituality is mostly relevant in our community, family, and love relationships.

Identity – Healthy Relationships – Boundaries

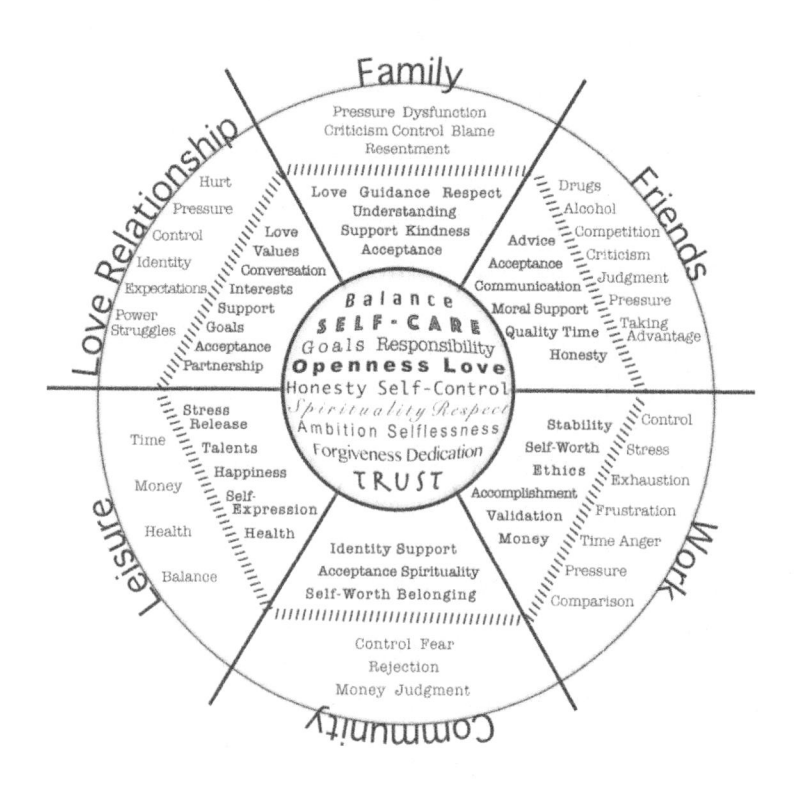

Family

Pressure Dysfunction
Criticism Control Blame
Resentment

Love Guidance Respect
Understanding
Support Kindness
Acceptance

Love Relationship

Hurt
Pressure
Control
Identity
Expectations
Power
Struggles

Love
Values
Conversation
Interests
Support
Goals
Acceptance
Partnership

Friends

Drugs
Alcohol
Competition
Criticism
Judgment
Pressure
Taking Advantage

Advice
Acceptance
Communication
Moral Support
Quality Time
Honesty

Center

Balance
SELF-CARE
Goals Responsibility
Openness Love
Honesty Self-Control
Spirituality Respect
Ambition Selflessness
Forgiveness Dedication
TRUST

Work

Stability
Self-Worth
Ethics
Accomplishment
Validation
Money

Control
Stress
Exhaustion
Frustration
Time Anger
Pressure
Comparison

Leisure

Stress
Release
Time
Money
Health
Balance

Talents
Happiness
Self-Expression
Health

Community

Identity Support
Acceptance Spirituality
Self-Worth Belonging

Control Fear
Rejection
Money Judgment

176

A blank, detachable copy of this diagram to explore our personal environment regarding benefits and needed boundaries can be found at the end of this book.

Overview of self-care ideas

This section combines the suggestions made throughout this book in no specific order in form of a condensed and easy to use list. A detachable copy of these self-care ideas can be found at the end of this book. We can keep it on the fridge, nightstand, bathroom mirror, our office desk, or the inside of our front door as a constant reminder of ways to improve our lives and that it is not as difficult as we might think. Having this list accessible makes it easier to do one thing for ourselves a day, learn a new coping skill a week, and create new habits that will ultimately make us happier.

Physical body

The following are merely suggestions on how to make healthier choices but do not replace a consultation with a registered dietitian or health care professional. Any changes in eating or exercise habits need to be made with our own specific health needs in mind.

➢ Replace processed foods with fresh home-cooked meals.
➢ Replace refined sugars with fruits and sweet vegetables.

- Look for healthy fats as found in seafood, nuts, seeds, avocados, and grass-fed meats.
- Replace refined wheat flour as in breads, pasta, and pizza with whole grains.
- Get enough protein as found in fish, chicken, beans, nuts, and seeds.
- Gradually replace GMOs with organic foods.
- Eat regular meals.
- Watch your portion size.
- Eat more slowly and chew more often.
- Get checked for food sensitivities.
- Search the internet for fast and easy recipes.
- Don't buy what you don't want to eat.
- Reduce your nicotine intake.
- Reduce your alcohol intake.
- Refrain from using recreational drugs.
- Reduce the use of electronics, especially before bedtime.
- Increase physical exercise as health permits.
- Find someone to exercise with.

Emotional body

- Avoid or reduce exposure to stressful situations.
- Evaluate the relationships in your life.
- Distinguish between needs and wants to get a grip on your finances.
- Be mindful of your exposure to the media.
- Have conversations without distractions of TV or phones.
- Spend time with loved ones and supportive people.

- Sit down with loved ones for dinner.
- Make your home environment happier.
- Clean out your home one room or one corner at a time.
- Put together a routine.
- Do one thing at a time.
- Find a hobby that brings you joy.
- Ask for help when you need help.
- Practice mindfulness or meditate often.
- Find joy in what you do.
- Appreciate more.
- Slow down your breathing, practice the 4-4-4-4 technique.
- Exercise and yoga help to relax.
- Use coping skills that involve any of your five senses:
  - Coloring, painting, sitting outside, watching funny shows, doing puzzles, reading stories, looking at photographs
  - Listening to music, listening to an audio book, playing an instrument
  - Using scented candles and essential oils
  - Eating food, cooking and baking
  - Working out, sweating, taking a shower or bath, getting a massage, getting a manicure or pedicure, getting some rest, practicing mindfulness

Mental body

- Control your negative thoughts: notice, acknowledge, push away, replace.

- Always watch the words you speak.
- Make positive self-statements.
- Focus on what you want, not on what you don't want.
- Accept yourself.
- Accept others.
- Avoid self-blame and self-pity, work on acceptance.
- Don't take things personally, see the bigger picture.
- Avoid what-ifs, look for solutions.
- Avoid expectations, ask for what you need.
- Communicate clearly.
- Avoid assumptions, ask what is really going on.
- Accept what you cannot change.
- Be grateful for who and what you have.
- Mindfulness slows down your thought processes and improves your focus.
- Choose to forgive others, not everything is your bag to carry.
- Do the best you can.

Spiritual body

- Work through old pain from the past.
- Avoid worries about the future.
- Learn to understand yourself and accept your own beliefs.
- Accept the beliefs of others.
- Find stillness in mindfulness and/or meditation.
- Be still and listen to figure out your purpose.
- Live your beliefs: pray, go to church, meditate, immerse yourself in nature.

- Focus on what is working.
- Be grateful and enjoy life.
- Stop complaining.
- Love yourself unconditionally every day.
- Love others unconditionally every day.
- Keep working on yourself to keep growing. We are never done.
- Help others.
- Establish healthy boundaries for unhealthy people.
- Ask questions and trust the answers you get.
- Be creative.

How to start self-care

Basically, we could pick one suggestion of each category at a time and work on that for a week. If we feel we don't need to work on a certain point because we are applying it already, we can check it off on our self-care ideas list. If we have worked on one skill and become pretty good at it, we can check that one off as well. If we feel we can work on more than one at a time, we can pick two. It is simple, and we can make it work for us. With every skill we work on, we will become more aware, more present in the moment, and healthier.

The following is one way to apply this list in our daily life:

Week 1

Pick one skill from each category and experiment with it. Remember that the physical body category has a nutrition and an exercise component, therefore, picking two skills from this section is recommended.

Physical body:

- **Eat regular meals.** We need to develop a routine, such as breakfast, lunch, dinner, one snack in the mornings, and one snack in the afternoons, make sure to not skip breakfast, and stop eating once we are full. We can stick to this routine for a week to start and then tailor it to what works for us as an individual.
- **Increase physical exercise as health permits.** If we have not done any exercise for a while, we can start with five minutes of walking or riding our bike, looking online for three Yoga poses that we would like to try out, doing five squats every night, doing five pushups against our bathroom sink before we shower, or using light dumbbells and exercising our arms. We can do one of these or more, or we can look for any exercise that may be suitable for us. We need to choose exercises that benefit us and not overdo them, otherwise we may get hurt and have to stop before we even had the chance to get started.

We need to always remember to consult our doctor in case we have any health issues that may not permit us to do certain physical exercises.

Emotional body:

> **Spend time with loved ones and supportive people.** We can go for lunch or coffee with friends, call on the phone to check in with them even if we only have five minutes available, or spend time with our spouse/partner/children daily even if it is only for half an hour, but we need to remember to turn the TV off and put our phone down. We need to be more aware of the people in our life and show them in one way or another that they matter.

Mental body:

> **Control your negative thoughts: notice, acknowledge, push away, replace.** This is a very crucial skill to learn, and it can be very tedious to change our thoughts. If we focus daily on what is going on in our heads and which negative thoughts we keep telling ourselves, we will become more and more aware of how our thoughts can make us miserable. We need to be honest with ourselves and acknowledge which thoughts we find in our minds. We have to learn to push the bad ones away and replace them with new thoughts. If we cannot come up with anything else but "I'm ok", that is

completely fine. If we run around all day long telling ourselves that we are okay, this alone can make a significant difference in the way we feel.

Spiritual body:

> **Find stillness in mindfulness and/or meditation.** Practicing being still is incredibly hard for many, but it is so crucial for our entire well-being. We can sit down in the morning for five minutes and enjoy our backyard, balcony, or a special place in our home. We could do the same in the evening or go for a walk during our lunch break, practicing mindfulness to shut off our thoughts. We can say a prayer and connect with our spirituality. We can use self-statements like "I'm a spiritual being", and meditate on how this statement feels in our body.

Weeks 2 + 3

Week 2 depends on how well we managed to stick to our plan in week 1. If we need to continue week 1 for another week, that is okay, if we feel that we managed to make subtle changes, we can build on them. The skills practiced in the following section will need at least two weeks to be mastered to the point of moving another step forward. Based on the suggestions above for week 1, week 2 + 3 can look as follows:

Physical body:

- **Watch your portion size.** In week 1, we practiced sticking to regular eating times, not skipping meals nor eating in addition to these times. We can now work on portion size and make sure we eat enough so we don't starve ourselves to lose weight, or we eat a little less if we need to.
- **Eat more slowly and chew more often.** This way we get full sooner and automatically eat less. Chewing more often aids digestion because more digestive enzymes make it into our food and help to break it up.
- Regarding **physical exercise** we may continue what we started the week before, work on being more consistent, or add five minutes to our workout. We can also change it up. If we walked the week before, we can do yoga poses now, or alternate between the two.

Emotional body:

- **Evaluate the relationships in your life.** We need to continue making efforts to spend time with loved ones and establish communication with family and friends we do not see on a regular basis. This does not need to change from the week prior. While we continue doing this, we can evaluate relationships in our lives and whether these conversations that we are seeking are in fact benefitting or harming us. Some relationships feel good and others don't. Some people we need more of in our lives, and with others we may need to set better boundaries. This is a good, and possibly painful, learning experience and may make us aware that we do not have to keep toxic people in our lives.

Mental body:

> ➤ **Keep working on controlling your thoughts.** This is an ongoing process that takes a lot of patience. We need to keep applying this skill consistently to create a new thinking habit.
> ➤ **Always watch the words you speak.** This skill goes hand in hand with controlling our thoughts. By using positive self-talk, we drown out negative thoughts, which helps to form our new thinking habit as well. Since thoughts come first and feelings follow, doing both these practices consistently may make us feel more positive and happier over all. Similarly, watching the words we speak to others is just as important. We need to avoid being negative, condescending, critical, or simply hurtful. We need to speak to others the way we would like them to speak to us. We want to point out what is working rather than focusing on everything they did wrong. We want to appreciate them for who they are rather than talking down on them and feeling superior. We want to support them and express our concerns matter-of-factly rather than criticizing what they do and how they do it. And we want to make others feel better rather than hurting them. Words have a lot of

power, we need to use them wisely. The way we address others always reflects on us. Therefore, talking down on others in any way will ultimately hurt us in regard to relationships and spirituality.

Spiritual body:

> **Continue practicing mindfulness and working on stillness.** As is the case with creating new thought processes, this skill needs a lot of practice and consistency. We need to keep looking for God, our Higher Power, a connection with nature, or an answer in science and be ready to find. Focusing on "finding" will bring us closer to our spirituality. If our focus is on "searching", our subconscious will continue the search rather than allowing us to find. We always need to look at what we are working towards as if we had it already, which makes reaching it much more likely. If we focus on wanting, we may end up wanting forever and never receive. If we focus on receiving, it is basically done.

Weeks 4 + 5

The skills for weeks 4 + 5 need to be focused on for more than a week as well in order to become more habitual and for us to be able to build on them. It is important to feel comfortable with the changes implemented so far, so we do not get overwhelmed when we consider adding an additional skill. All changes discussed are lifestyle changes and do not happen quickly nor easily at all. But every single one can become a habit and can eventually be accomplished automatically. At the same time, our choices in general become healthier in the process as well.

Physical body:

> **Replace refined sugars with fruits and sweet vegetables.** Having established our eating routine, determining a good portion size for us, and chewing our meals properly, we can begin to consider whether we need to change what we are eating. Watching our sugar intake is just one possibility of many. We can read labels to figure out how much we are really ingesting daily, reduce the number of desserts we eat during a week, reduce the sodas we drink every day, eat fruits instead of cake, or experiment with sweet vegetables and see if they can reduce our sugar cravings. Since sugar has been linked to so many lifestyle diseases this is a good starting point to explore how healthy our diet really is. Of course, as with every other nutrition related suggestion in this book, consult a registered dietitian if you decide to change your eating habits to make sure that your body is still receiving all the nutrients it needs every day.
> **Find someone to exercise with.** We can continue our exercise by ourselves, but we could also ask our spouse, partner, or a friend to exercise with us. We can start riding bikes, hiking, skating, or rock climbing with our children. We can join a yoga class

or meetup group that is active in nature. This will make it easier to stick to a routine. We can check out a gym, they offer classes but working out on our own is an option too, or we could hire a personal trainer to get a routine started. If we continue our exercises at home, we can continue what we have been doing or build on that. It is important not to put too much pressure on ourselves by adding too much exercise all at once because this may backfire to the point that we could quit exercise altogether, which we want to avoid.

Emotional body:

➢ **Slow down your breathing, use the 4-4-4-4 technique.** Breathing is vital to achieve stillness and relaxation. We only need to do the 4-4-4-4 technique for a couple minutes at a time but can do it a few times during the day. We also need to remember to take a deep breath regularly because our breathing is usually very shallow, and we literally seem to forget to breathe. We can use humor and put a reminder on our phone every hour that says: "breathe". Then we simply smile and do it.

Mental body:

➢ **Accept others.** We have been working on our relationships for three or four weeks and can now focus on accepting others where they are, even if we don't agree with their choices. We can decide to refrain from criticizing them or trying to fix what they are doing wrong in our eyes. We can use self-statements such as "I choose to accept them, I don't have to like what they do", and we can express our concerns matter-of-factly and listen to and acknowledge their response, but then it is important to drop the conversation before it ends in an argument. We don't wait for them to take our advice and change what they do right away. In fact, they may never. This is great practice to stay focused on our own lives and not on those of others. We also need to refrain from talking negatively about anyone else behind their backs. Gossip and rumors are destructive and hurtful in nature and simply reflect poorly on our own character. We simply have no right to judge others on where they are and how they live their lives. Most likely, they live their lives to the best of their abilities as well, just like us.

Spiritual body:

➢ **Live your beliefs: pray, go to church, meditate, immerse yourself in nature.** Even if we don't know for sure what we believe, we can get involved in spiritual communities in order to learn. We can start with praying regularly. We can also find a church and see how we feel in that environment. If we don't feel comfortable, we can look for another one and compare. We can visit different churches until we find one that fits our needs. We can also start exploring various religions and study them, comparing what they are about and what resonates most with us. We can hug a tree and try to feel its energy. We need to live what we know or try out and research if we don't know enough. Whatever we do, wherever we are, it has to work for us and does not depend on anyone else.

How to finetune and build on existing self-care

If we feel that we already have basic self-care in place, we need to assess first where we are in terms of nutrition, physical exercise, our emotional state, mental state, and spiritual practice. Do we eat healthy and regular meals, do we eat fresh or processed foods, do we have enough carbohydrates, protein, fats, vitamins, and minerals in our diet in form of fresh foods, fruits, vegetables, and grass-fed meats? Do we exercise regularly, do we include cardio and strengthening exercises, and is our exercise balanced to benefit our body? How are we doing emotionally: do we have mood swings, irritability, depressed mood, and anxiety or are we balanced and in control of our feelings? How are we doing in regard to our thought processes: are we able to control our thoughts, are we able to distinguish between fear-based, emotional thinking and logical thinking, do we manage to avoid expectations and assumptions, can we accept ourselves and others, and are we able to have productive conversations even about personal and emotional topics? And finally, do we feel safe in our spirituality, do we feel connected and authentic in our beliefs, and do we know how to practice our spirituality to make us feel whole?

We need to be honest to ourselves about what we really do for our self-care, whether we are making enough time to be consistent in our efforts, whether we are content and happy where we are in life, and whether our efforts really work or not. We can always change and adjust what is not working, but we need to admit first that something is amiss, even if we cannot put our finger on it and have no clue what this could possibly be. We need to watch out for self-criticism and that negative voice that just loves to put us down because it can wreck any self-care effort we may attempt. We also need to establish a routine that works for us and that is balanced with regard to the four bodies as well as our work and family life, because somehow everything has to fit into a 24-hour day.

The foregoing section about how to start self-care when you have not done anything for some time has put the following aspects into our daily routine:

Physical body: Eating regular meals, watching portion size, eating more slowly and chewing more, replacing refined sugars with fresh fruit and sweet vegetables, as well as choosing five minutes of whatever kind of exercise and building on it, possibly alternating various exercises, and finding someone to exercise with.

Emotional body: Spending time with loved ones and supportive people, evaluating relationships in our lives, and slowing down our breathing and taking deeper breaths.

Mental body: Controlling our thoughts, learning to replace negative thoughts, watching the words we speak to ourselves as well as others, and accepting others the way they are.

Spiritual body: Finding stillness in mindfulness or meditation, listening to the stillness to find our spirituality, and living our beliefs such as trying out churches if we have not found one yet and we feel the need to do so, researching religions, praying, or hugging trees.

While all these tools may have felt overwhelming when incorporating them in our daily lives at the very beginning, they may feel easier and more habitual by now. They are a good foundation to build on and the following section is making suggestions on how to continue from here:

Physical body:

- Focus on cooking fresh home-cooked meals and finding one new recipe on a weekly basis.
- Incorporate healthy carbohydrates, proteins, and fats in our diets.

- Research GMOs and consider whether going organic would work for you.
- Get checked for food sensitivities.
- Don't buy what you don't want to eat.
- Evaluate your nicotine/alcohol/drug use and consider making positive changes.
- Evaluate your use of electronics and consider making positive changes.
- Keep building on or maintaining a healthy exercise routine.
- Consult with your doctor, registered dietitian or personal trainer to make the best choices regarding nutrition and exercise.

Emotional body:

- Avoid stressful situations at home or at work – change what is not working.
- Distinguish between needs and wants to get a grip on your finances.
- Be mindful of your exposure to the media.
- Work on your home environment, clean up, get rid of stuff.
- Consider whether a daily routine would work for you.
- Consider how you could improve your work environment (work space, relationships).
- Find a hobby, have fun.
- Ask for help.

- Practice mindfulness often.
- Appreciate who and what you have.
- Use coping skills involving your five senses.

Mental body:

- Focus on what you want, not on what you don't want.
- Avoid self-blame and self-pity, work on acceptance.
- Don't take things personally, see the bigger picture.
- Avoid what-ifs, find solutions.
- Avoid expectations, ask for what you need.
- Work on communicating effectively.
- Avoid assumptions, clarify your concerns.
- Accept what you cannot change.
- Be grateful for who and what you have.
- Learn to forgive.
- Do the best you can.

Spiritual body:

- Let go of the past.
- Don't worry about the future, work towards it.
- Practice gratitude.
- Love yourself.
- Love others.
- Keep growing.
- Help others.
- Establish healthy boundaries.
- Be creative.

As I have mentioned before, we need to work on one skill or change at a time. This can be with the help of a professional or if we feel we have enough knowledge and insight, we can start tackling these points on our own. The mental body suggestions include challenges that are best addressed with the help of a professional counselor. Some of the suggestions for the physical body may require the help of a registered dietitian or professional trainer. It is perfectly okay to get help, especially if accepting it brings us closer to our goal: feeling well, being healthy in our body, mind, and spirit, and finding happiness.

Conclusion

Many people suffer from illnesses, need daily medications, and do not feel well in their own skin. They struggle with weight issues and in their emotional and mental life, feel constant stress, and are not as happy as they could possibly be. Many of these concerns, however, seem to be linked to lifestyle choices. Saying that, I strongly believe that changing the way we live our lives can improve our quality of life drastically.

My goal for this book was to make it very clear that we must keep ourselves healthy physically, emotionally, mentally, and spiritually to find happiness in life. All four levels impact each other, sometimes greatly and sometimes subtly. But they do so because all four levels are simply four parts of one – YOU. The beauty in the matter is that YOU can do a lot to become healthier and happier, but it requires consistent work and sometimes profound changes. We need to learn new ways of daily living and consistency is key. There is no band aid solution. We cannot "fix the problem" for two weeks and then turn back to our old ways and expect to be okay. We need to create new and lasting habits that simply make sense to us, because they make us feel so much better than we used to that we do not ever want to go back to our old ways.

Considering the complexity of well-being and self-improvement as discussed in this book, it is obvious that consulting professionals on the road to health and happiness may be the way to go. That said, it is also obvious that we need to achieve greater cooperation among health professionals, educators, yoga and fitness instructors, as well as spiritual and religious leaders. A more comprehensive training for professionals may be necessary to provide holistic support and treatment. Ignorance is never an excuse, and the helping professions need to make sure to receive the best education possible not only in their own specialty but also in fields that may impact their work. It can be beneficial for psychotherapists to also address their clients' physical and spiritual issues in their treatment, just like physical therapists may find that understanding their patients' nutritional and emotional struggles can increase the effectiveness of their work. The medical community could put greater focus on the impact of their patients' diet and mental stress on their physical health, while teachers who embrace a holistic perspective might learn to understand their students better when they present with mood issues, hyperactivity, and attention problems.

I have discussed the impact of the food we eat not just on our physical health but also on the way we feel in every chapter to show which aspect of our diet affects our physical, emotional, and mental health respectively the most. It may seem very overwhelming to focus on how every food and every deficiency appear to affect our brain, but even simple changes in our diet can have big effects on our health. We don't need to know every chemical reaction in our body to live healthy. That's why there are professionals whom we can consult when we need to. But we can prioritize and focus on a couple things that we choose to implement from now on, such as cooking fresh foods at home as often as possible and finding ways to prepare it fast, make it last, and especially make it healthy and still tasty. We can focus on reducing the sugar in our diet, finding alternatives to snack on, and changing our sugar habits that have taken over and seem to make our society very sick. And we can watch how often we eat white flour products and find ways of replacing these with whole grains or other nutritious dishes that fit our individual needs.

The importance to keep our physical body healthy seems to be obvious. In addition to food, exercise is the other component we need to incorporate into our daily lives for our physical health. Our bodies are not meant to be sedentary, they need to move. We don't need to be bodybuilders or serious athletes, but we also don't need to be couch potatoes. Somewhere in the middle is the right amount for all of us, and we need to find out what our bodies need to remain healthy and strong.

Food related emotional issues, relationships, work, stress, and the need for joy and fun in life directly affect the way we feel. The people we allow into our lives need to be good for us, we can let everyone else go. We need to learn to build solid boundaries to those people in our lives who will always be there due to familial or work circumstances but who are toxic to us nevertheless.

There are ways to keep ourselves safe, and we need to figure out what works for us. Any type of chronic stress in our lives is detrimental and causes health issues on all levels. Learning to deal with stress by managing our time, balancing our lives, organizing our environments, and making choices regarding the people around us is a major component on our path to health and happiness. We cannot expect to keep living through multiple stresses every day and being able to maintain our physical, emotional, mental, and spiritual health.

Mental health naturally depends on brain chemistry quite a bit, but the thoughts we think are the other big culprit of mental health issues that often seems to be overlooked. How brain chemistry is affected by food choices has been discussed, so have ways to reduce our mental stress and negativity, change our perspectives of ourselves, others, and the world in general, and learn to accept and find gratitude. Making changes to how we eat and think will improve mental health symptoms in a great number of people. For some it will take care of most, or even all, of their symptoms; for others it will make it easier to manage their mental health challenges. Whichever the outcome, there is help and alleviation, and it is up to us to go and grab it.

And finally, I addressed the importance of spirituality. Some have found their path and know how to live their spirituality, others are searching. Whichever it is, it is okay. We need to accept where we are, and we need to allow ourselves to go on our personal spiritual journey to find love and peace in our core. We need to accept and find love for ourselves and others, no matter what their spiritual beliefs may be. Learning not to judge together with being loving and accepting will set us free in our hearts and minds on our path to find happiness.

Putting all these elements together and creating your own self-care routine based on the sample action plan in this book is a choice that you can make. What happens next is only up to you, so is putting the work in to become a healthier and happier you. I hope you see that there is a whole lot that you can do starting today. I also hope that you love yourself enough to not only get started, but also continue the work one change at a time. This journey you are on doesn't just benefit you, it benefits everyone that you love around you as well, because they finally get to know the better, healthier, and happier you as well. Everyone wins.

About the Author

Alexandra M. Asirvadam grew up in a small town in southeastern Austria. After graduating from high school, she moved to Vienna to study both the English and Spanish languages and literature and graduated with her first Master's degree from the University of Vienna, while working two jobs. In 1997, she moved to England and obtained her Master's degree in Marketing Management from Southampton Institute. In 1998, she returned to Vienna to work as a Marketing Assistant, but moved to Dallas, Texas one year later after getting married. Her husband's contract work took the couple to Ireland for a year and to Slovenia for another. They had two boys, and in 2005, when her older son started Kindergarten, she returned to school to get her Master's degree in Professional Counseling from Argosy University in Dallas, following an inner voice that told her to help people overcome abuse and trauma. She had a baby girl after graduating, and worked for a mental health hospital and a foster care agency until she started her private practice in 2011. She studied various approaches to healing trauma and has successfully helped many clients to work through their past experiences and mental health issues and re-establish themselves in the present. When she realized how much mental health is affected by the food we eat, she also got a certification as an Integrative Nutrition Health Coach from the Institute of Integrative Nutrition to learn more about the body-brain connection and be able to assist her clients better in making healthier choices in their everyday life. She is dedicated to improving the approach to treating mental health issues, adopting a more holistic perspective, so clients can live happier and healthier lives.

Notes

Moving mental health counseling to the next level
1. Myers, Fall 2008; Roscoe, Spring 2009

The physical body
1. Notaras Murphy, February 2013
2. Hyman, 67
3. Hyman, 73
4. Hyman, 59
5. Nematollahi, 2017
6. Notaras Murphy, February 2013
7. Hyman, 62
8. Hyman, 63
9. Amen, 72-73
10. Amen, 29
11. Amen, 40
12. Schure, Winter 2008
13. Shallcross, October 2012

The emotional body
1. Hyman, 56
2. Pearson, Winter 2008
3. Heim, 2013
4. Idell
5. Ivey, December 2009; Peterson, February 2012
6. McKennon, 2017

The mental body
1. Psychology Today, July/August 2013
2. Lim, 2016
3. Psychology Today, January/February 2016
4. Psychology Today, May/June 2012 and May/June 2016

5. Lim, 2016
6. Banikazemi, 2016
7. Psychology Today, September/October 2012
8. Lim, 2016
9. Hyman, 147
10. Nguyen, 2017
11. Bishwajit, 2017
12. Hyman, 58
13. Nematollahi, 2017
14. Perlmutter, 66-67, 85-87
15. Perlmutter, 99
16. Korn, 45
17. Psychology Today, July/August 2017 and November/December 2015
18. Yoshikawa, 2016
19. Hyman, 57
20. Hyman, 97
21. Psychology Today, September/October 2015
22. Psychology Today, November/December 2012
23. Hyman, 189
24. Korn, 128
25. Psychology Today, May/June 2017
26. Psychology Today, July/August 2016
27. Psychology Today, March/April 2014
28. Jacka, 2017
29. Jacka, 2017
30. Hyman, 12
31. Hyman, 50-51
32. Psychology Today, September/October 2012
33. Hyman, 21
34. Jacka, 2017
35. Hyman, 27
36. Hyman, 55

37. Hyman, 17
38. Shallcross, October 2012
39. Shallcross, January 2012

The spiritual body
1. Hillaire, September 2010
2. Schulte, January 2012
3. Bowers, October 2012

Resources

Amen, D (1998, 2015). *Change your brain, change your life (revised and expanded, Kindle edition).* New York: Harmony Books.

Banikazemi, Z., Mirzaei, H., Mokhber, N. & Mobarhan, M. G. (2016, March). Selenium intake is related to Beck's Depression Score [Electronic version]. *Iranian Red Crescent Medical Journal, 18(3),* e21993.

Bishwajit, G., O'Leary, D. P., Ghosh, S., Sanni, Y., Shangfeng, T. & Zhanchun, F. (2017). Association between depression and fruit and vegetable consumption among adults in South Asia [Electronic version]. *BMC Psychiatry, 17,* 15.

Bowers, R. (October 2012). Clinical knowledge and spiritual wisdom: a beacon in the darkness. *Counseling Today,* 14-16.

Chu-Lien Chao, R. (Summer 2011). Managing stress and maintaining well-being: social support, problem-focused coping, and avoidant coping. *Journal of Counseling & Development, 89,* 338-348).

Corey, G. (2005). *Theory and practice of counseling & psychotherapy* (7th ed.). Belmont, CA: Brooks/Cole – Thomson Learning.

Cummins, R. & Lilliston, B. (2000). *Genetically engineered food.* New York: Marlowe & Company.

Davidson, J. (March/April 2014). The psychobiotic revolution. *Psychology Today,* 40-41.

Eden, D. & Feinstein, D. (1998). *Energy Medicine.* New York: Jeremy P. Tarcher/Putnam.

Estroff Marano, H. (May/June 2012). The vanishing mineral. *Psychology Today,* 42.

Estroff Marano, H. (September/October 2012). The trouble with fructose. *Psychology Today,* 48.

Estroff Marano, H. (November/December 2012). Food chain. *Psychology Today,* 48-49.

Estroff Marano, H. (November/December 2015). Ich bin ein Fathead. *Psychology Today,* 33-34.

Estroff Marano, H. (January/February 2016). Seeing the light on vitamin D. *Psychology Today,* 29-30.

Estroff Marano, H. (May/June 2016). An element of protection. *Psychology Today,* 29-30.

Estroff Marano, H. (May/June 2017). A bug in the system. *Psychology Today,* 31-32.

Goldynia, K. (July/August 2017). How signals get skewed. *Psychology Today,* 29-30.

Goodrick, K. (2/27/2012). *Food for thought: How nutrients affect mental health and the brain. A seminar for health professionals and educators.* Sponsored by Institute for Brain Potential.

Hansen, J. T. (Summer 2007). Should counseling be considered a health care profession? Critical thoughts on the transition to a health care ideology. *Journal of Counseling & Development, 85,* 286-292.

Hay, L. L. (1984). *You can heal your life.* Carlsbad, CA, New York City: Hay House, Inc..

Hyman, M. (2009). *The UltraMind Solution.* New York: Scribner.

Idell, R. & Nemeroff, C. B.. The neurobiology of child abuse and neglect. *Hatherleigh.* Retrieved July 14, 2017 from https://www.scribd.com/document/264253829/tmpC583-tmp.

Ivey, A., Bradford Ivey, M., Zalaquett, C. & Quirk K. (December 2009). Counseling and neuroscience: the cutting edge of the coming decade. *Counseling Today,* 44-48.

Jacka, F. N. (2017 March). Nutritional Psychiatry: Where to next? [Electronic version]. *EBioMedicine, 17,* 24-29.

Kabat-Zinn, J. (1990). *Full catastrophe living. Using the wisdom of your body and mind to face stress, pain, and illness.* New York: Bantam Books Trade Paperbacks.

Kabat-Zinn, J. (2012). *Mindfulness for beginners. Reclaiming the present moment – and your life.* Boulder, CO: Sounds True, Inc..

Korn, L. (2016). *Nutrition essentials for mental health. A complete guide to the food-mood connection.* New York: W. W. Norton & Company, Inc..

Leanza, N. (October 2012). Simple therapeutic interventions for rewiring the maladaptive brain. *Counseling Today,* 54-55.

Lim, S. Y., Kim, E. J, Kim, A., Lee, H. J., Choi, H. J. & Yang, S. J (2016, July). Nutritional factors affecting mental health [Electronic version]. *Clinical Nutrition Research, 5(3),* 143-152.

Lipton, B. H. (2005). *The biology of belief: Unleashing the power of consciousness, matter & miracles* (2nd ed.). Carlsbad, CA, New York City: Hay House Inc..

Marano, D. A. (September/October 2015). Taking root. *Psychology Today,* 37-38.

McKennon, S., Levitt, S. E. & Bulaj, G. (2017). Commentary: A breathing-based meditation intervention for patients with major depressive disorder following inadequate response to antidepressants: a randomized pilot study [Electronic version]. *Frontiers in Medicine, 4,* 37.

Myers, J. E. & Sweeney, T. J. (Fall 2008). Wellness counseling: the evidence base for practice. *Journal of Counseling & Development, 86,* 482-492.

Nematollahi, S, Keshteli, A. H., Esmaillzadeh, A., Roohafza, H., Afshar, H., Adibi, P. et al. (2017). The mediating role of mental health in the relationship between dietary behaviors and general health: a cross-sectional study [Electronic version]. *Advanced Biomedical Research, 6,* 21.

Nguyen, B., Ding, D. & Mihrshahi, S. (2017). Fruit and vegetable consumption and psychological distress: cross-sectional and longitudinal analyses based on a large Australian sample [Electronic version]. *BMJ Open, 7(3),* e014201.

Notaras Murphy, S. (February 2013). Are you what you eat? *Counseling Today,* 40-44.

Pearson, Q. M. (Winter 2008). Role overload, job satisfaction, leisure satisfaction, and psychological health among employed women. *Journal of Counseling & Development, 86,* 57-64.

Pease Banitt, S. (2012). *The trauma tool kit. Healing PTSD from the inside out.* Wheaton: Quest Books.

Perlmutter, D. & Loberg, K (2013). *Grain brain. The surprising truth about wheat, carbs and sugar – your brain's silent killers.* New York: Little, Brown and Company.

Peterson, A. (February, 2012). Bringing mindfulness into your counseling practice. *Counseling Today*, 46-49.

Roscoe, L. J. (Spring 2009). Wellness: a review of theory and measurement for counselors. *Journal of Counseling & Development, 87,* 216-226.

Ruiz, D. M. (1997). *The four agreements.* San Rafael, CA: Amber-Allen Publishing.

Shallcross, L. (January 2012). The benefits of forgiveness and gratitude. *Counseling Today,* 42-45.

Shallcross, L. (February 2012). A calming presence. *Counseling Today,* 28-39.

Shallcross, L. (October 2012). Where east meets west. *Counseling Today,* 28-37.

Schulte, R. A. (January 2012). The art of noticing: being mindful of how the losses of life affect us. *Counseling Today,* 50-53.

Schure, M. B., Christopher, J. & Christopher S. (Winter 2008). Mind-body medicine and the art of self-care: teaching mindfulness to counseling students through Yoga, meditation, and Qigong. *Journal of Counseling & Development, 86,* 47-56.

St. Hillaire, A. (September 2010). Addressing spiritual diversity. *Counseling Today,* 48-49.

Stevens, A. J., Rucklidge, J. J. & Kennedy, M. A (2017 May). Epigenetics, nutrition and mental health. Is there a relationship [Electronic version]. *Nutritional Neuroscience, 29*, 1-12.

Swaminathan, N. (September/October 2012). Stealth attack. *Psychology Today*, 78-86.

University of Miami (2013, June 1). Specific changes in brain structure after different forms of child abuse. *ScienceDaily*. Retrieved June 10, 2013, from http://www.sciencedaily.com/releases/2013/06/130601133735.htm?utm_source=feedburner&utm_medium=feed&utm_campaign=Feed%3A+sciencedaily+%28ScienceDaily%3A+Latest+Science+News%29.

Wenner Moyer, M. (July/August 2013). The Queen B. *Psychology Today*, 46-47.

White, J. (July/August 2016). Going with the gut. *Psychology Today*, 35-36.

Yoshikawa, E., Nishi, D. & Matsuoka, Y. J. (2016). Association between frequency of fried food consumption and resilience to depression in Japanese company workers: a cross-sectional study [Electronic version]. *Lipids in Health and Disease, 15*, 156.

Ziegler, D.. Impacting the brain of the traumatized child. *Jasper Mountain*. Retrieved July 14, 2017, from www.jaspermountain.org/impacting_brain_traumatized_child.pdf.

Identity – Healthy Relationships – Boundaries

Explore relationships in your life and the boundaries you need to set.

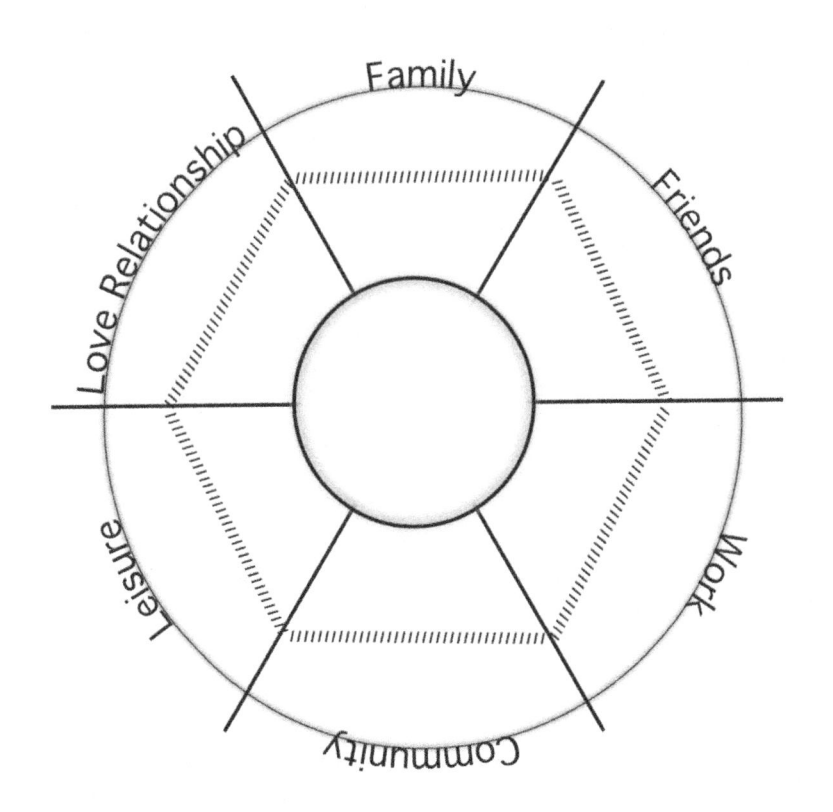

.

Physical body

- ☐ Replace processed foods with fresh home-cooked meals.
- ☐ Replace refined sugars with fruits and sweet vegetables.
- ☐ Look for healthy fats as found in seafood, nuts, seeds, avocados, and grass-fed meats.
- ☐ Replace refined wheat flour as in breads, pasta, and pizza with whole grains.
- ☐ Get enough protein as found in fish, chicken, beans, nuts, and seeds.
- ☐ Gradually replace GMOs with organic foods.
- ☐ Eat regular meals.
- ☐ Watch your portion size.
- ☐ Eat more slowly and chew more often.
- ☐ Get checked for food sensitivities.
- ☐ Search the internet for fast and easy recipes.
- ☐ Don't buy what you don't want to eat.
- ☐ Reduce your nicotine intake.
- ☐ Reduce your alcohol intake.
- ☐ Refrain from using recreational drugs.
- ☐ Reduce the use of electronics, especially before bedtime.
- ☐ Increase physical exercise as health permits.
- ☐ Find someone to exercise with.

Emotional body

- ☐ Avoid or reduce exposure to stressful situations.
- ☐ Evaluate the relationships in your life.
- ☐ Distinguish between needs and wants to get a grip on your finances.
- ☐ Be mindful of your exposure to the media.
- ☐ Have conversations without distractions of TV or phones.
- ☐ Spend time with loved ones and supportive people.
- ☐ Sit down with loved ones for dinner.
- ☐ Make your home environment happier.
- ☐ Clean out your home one room or one corner at a time.
- ☐ Put together a routine.
- ☐ Do one thing at a time.
- ☐ Find a hobby that brings you joy.
- ☐ Ask for help when you need help.
- ☐ Practice mindfulness or meditate often.
- ☐ Find joy in what you do.
- ☐ Appreciate more.
- ☐ Slow down your breathing, practice the 4-4-4 technique.
- ☐ Exercise and yoga help to relax.
- ☐ Use coping skills that involve any of your five senses.

Mental body

- ☐ Control your negative thoughts: notice, acknowledge, push away, replace.
- ☐ Always watch the words you speak.
- ☐ Make positive self-statements.
- ☐ Focus on what you want, not on what you don't want.
- ☐ Accept yourself.
- ☐ Accept others.
- ☐ Avoid self-blame and self-pity, work on acceptance.
- ☐ Don't take things personally, see the bigger picture.
- ☐ Avoid what-ifs, look for solutions.
- ☐ Avoid expectations, ask for what you need.
- ☐ Communicate clearly.
- ☐ Avoid assumptions, ask what is really going on.
- ☐ Accept what you cannot change.
- ☐ Be grateful for who and what you have.
- ☐ Mindfulness slows down your thought processes and improves your focus.
- ☐ Choose to forgive others, not everything is your bag to carry.
- ☐ Do the best you can.

Spiritual body

- ☐ Work through old pain from the past.
- ☐ Avoid worries about the future.
- ☐ Learn to understand yourself and accept your own beliefs.
- ☐ Accept the beliefs of others.
- ☐ Find stillness in mindfulness and/or meditation.
- ☐ Be still and listen to figure out your purpose.
- ☐ Live your beliefs: pray, go to church, meditate, immerse yourself in nature.
- ☐ Focus on what is working.
- ☐ Be grateful and enjoy life.
- ☐ Stop complaining.
- ☐ Love yourself unconditionally every day.
- ☐ Love others unconditionally every day.
- ☐ Keep working on yourself to keep growing. We are never done.
- ☐ Help others.
- ☐ Establish healthy boundaries for unhealthy people.
- ☐ Ask questions and trust the answers you get.
- ☐ Be creative.

Made in the USA
Coppell, TX
21 February 2022